HOW TO WRITE THE WINNING BRIEF

Strategies for

Effective Memoranda,

Briefs,

Client Letters,

and Other

Legal Documents

Frederic G. Gale
and
Joseph M. Moxley

Section of General Practice American Bar Association

Printed in the United States of America.

Library of Congress Catalog Card Number 92-54504
ISBN 0-89707-828-4

97 96 5 4 3 2

ABOUT THE AUTHORS

Fredric G. Gale (J.D., Ph.D.) has been a practicing attorney for more than twenty years, during which time he has acted as general counsel of a corporation listed on the New York Stock Exchange and served as a judge in a Wisconsin state court. Gale has been a member of the American, Wisconsin, Milwaukee, and Chicago Bar Associations. He has published a number of articles and has been editor and publisher of a financial newsletter. Gale presently teaches legal and professional writing at the University of Arkansas, as well as graduate courses in composition and rhetoric.

Joseph M. Moxley (Ph.D.) teaches legal writing at Stetson University College of Law. An associate professor of English at the University of South Florida, he also teaches workshops on scholarly publishing for university faculty and graduate English courses in composition and rhetoric. In 1990, he received a Florida Board of Regents Award for Excellence in Undergraduate Teaching.

Moxley has published numerous academic articles and served as an editor for several academic journals. Other books published by Moxley include *Publish, Don't Perish: The Scholar's Guide to Academic Writing and Publishing; Creative Writing in America: Theory and Pedagogy;* and *Writing and Publishing for Academic Authors.*

Gale and Moxley are comanaging partners of Communication Process Associates, a consulting firm that specializes in legal and professional writing. Gale and Moxley are available to lead legal writing workshops based on the strategies illustrated in this book.

Acknowledgments

We are particularly indebted to Susan Yessne for her constant encouragement. In addition, we thank Beverly Loder and Janet Battiste for their thoughtful comments and careful copyediting. For helping us develop realistic writing samples and documents, we also thank attorneys Paul Moxley and Janet Macnab.

CONTENTS

Introduction

Writing, Thinking, and the Practice of Law

To be a successful lawyer, you must distinguish fact from opinion, scrutinize human behavior to understand why others act as they do, conduct research to find evidence to support your assertions, organize persuasive arguments, and apply legal principles. Yet all of these fundamental skills are overshadowed by one dominant requirement: you must be capable of articulating your ideas in writing. Judges, clients, and other lawyers base their perception of your competence largely on how well you write. A substantial part of your day is dedicated to drafting ideas in written form. In fact, William Prosser, the author of a number of books on negligence, once remarked that "the average lawyer writes more than the average novelist."

Being able to communicate complicated ideas and sway readers through shrewd reasoning and persuasive appeals is clearly a powerful reason for working on your writing. Yet thanks to the research of scholars in the fields of linguistics, cognitive psychology, and composition and rhetoric, we now understand that writing allows us to do much more than communicate: *writing is a generative, thought-provoking process*. Instead of assuming that writers always should know what they will say before writing, we now understand that writers use various prewriting, drafting, revising, collaborating, and editing strategies to help them discover, develop, and polish ideas. We know that writing enhances comprehension and recall and that it gives ideas a sense of permanence and perspective. We know that time spent revising our work promotes analysis and synthesis and that our ideas can best be evaluated once they are written. We know that it is far easier to reexamine, confirm, or refute our ideas once they are stated boldly on the page, rather than merely floating around in our minds.

The assumption that writing shapes thinking represents a radical departure from the previous generation's assumptions about the role of writing and thinking. In the past, it was assumed that people thought in a nonlinguistic form—through images, feelings, bodily sensations. This view of thinking assumed that knowledge existed in a "pure form" within us. According to this view, language reflected thoughts rather than generating them. Consequently, people considered writing to be a purely ornamental skill, and law schools thought it unnecessary to emphasize writing in their curriculum. When instructors or textbook authors discussed writing, they typically encouraged students to look deep within themselves and to think through their ideas before writing. Authorities asked students to write thesis statements or outlines prior to actually composing a rough draft. Until recently, prewriting and drafting activities were rarely mentioned by writing teachers or textbooks, and the important distinctions between revising and editing were rarely discussed. Instead, teachers assumed that students could learn how to develop texts by studying manuscripts written by professionals or by studying grammar and usage rules.

Our newfound knowledge of how writers generate and revise documents has forced us to reconsider the role of writing in legal interpretation. Instead of assuming that you should do extensive research and then write or that you should know everything you plan on saying before writing, we now know that writing, thinking, and the legal interpretive method are thoroughly interrelated.

As Peter Elbow has argued in *Embracing Contraries*, you can better harness the generative aspect of writing by balancing *believing* with *doubting*.[1] Throughout this book, we show you how to achieve this balance in order to write more effective documents in less time. Based on recent composition research, we suggest that you need to set aside your role as skeptic when first beginning a writing project and play the *believing game*. Instead of encouraging you to be a tough editor who harshly critiques drafts or ideas in their infancy, we encourage you temporarily to embrace the attitude that even your weakest ideas will find support through the thinking and revising process. And once you have developed a substantive draft—one that takes into account your audience, purpose, and tone—we show you how to play the *doubting game* and to look at your writing critically. Yet, instead of

1. Peter Elbow. *Embracing Contraries*. New York: Oxford University Press, 1986.

suggesting that you should ask every question that comes to mind, we show you how to systematize the revision process so that you focus on the most substantive concerns first.

How This Book Is Organized

We have divided this book into four sections. In Part I, we show you diverse ways to plan and draft documents. If you find yourself writing legal documents at the last minute or if it takes you so long to complete the first draft that you do not have sufficient time to revise—even if you have some good ideas for improving a manuscript—then you will find the drafting and organizing strategies discussed in these opening chapters to be particularly useful. The strategies should help you get a good start for any writing task.

To show how to use the writing process to develop ideas and interpretations, we have organized Part II of this book around a *unified case study method*. This approach allows us to clarify how your writing is affected by the conventions of legal practice, the particular requirements of the law firm, the sometimes adverse demands of judges and opposing counsel, and the needs and purposes of the client. We ask you to play the role of an attorney in a law firm that represents the plaintiff in a fictitious case. In turn, to give you a stronger sense of how your audience influences what and how you write, we ask you on occasion to play the role of the attorney for one of the defendants.

The facts and laws involved in the case unfold as you move through the text, just as lawyers handling a real case will develop facts and law as they work on the case. By the end of Part II, you will have had the opportunity to examine the process of writing seven documents of increasing difficulty in the same chronological order as you might have to write them in a real situation. Although the example is for a negligence case, the writing principles employed are equally applicable to all of the writing you need to do as a lawyer, including writing quick notes to colleagues, formal letters, memoranda, letters, opinions, briefs, statements to a jury, law review articles, and so on.

You will want to refer to the chapters in Part III if you have difficulties organizing your work. These chapters review the conventions for introducing documents, organizing the body of expository and persuasive documents, and writing conclusions.

Have you ever wondered whether any consensus exists about the standards of effective legal writing and writing in general? Are you unsure about how to improve documents or concerned that you actually make your documents worse with revision? If so, then you will find the chapters in Part IV to be especially useful. By practicing the revising and copyediting strategies discussed in these chapters, you can be sure that your documents carry the necessary knockout punch. We present over two dozen techniques that can help you critique a document and correct underdeveloped thinking or imprecise and wordy prose.

Final Comments

You can improve your writing if you challenge yourself to write regularly and explore the numerous techniques illustrated in this book. At first the prewriting, drafting, revising, and copyediting techniques may seem awkward. All of us have difficulties trying new techniques. Yet what at first may appear to be a simplistic idea can be a lifesaver once you begin to implement it. With extensive practice, you can develop innovative ideas, synthesize complex information, incorporate evidence and support for your position, and use sound reasoning and even emotional appeals to convince other people about the value of your thinking. If you truly take our suggestions to heart, over time, you will, we are sure, write as successfully as winning lawyers do.

PART I

The Believing Game: Beginning the Writing Process

CHAPTER 1

Saving Time by Prewriting

Obviously, in your busy life, you must treat procrastination as the enemy. You cannot permit yourself to put writing projects off to the last minute. Nevertheless, this does not mean that you should always dive in and then expect to refine and polish your manuscript through numerous revisions. Naturally, leaping before looking can work well if you have addressed a similar purpose and audience before and know exactly the form your document should take. Extensive planning can be unnecessary when you know the likely terrain before you.

However, if you are writing about a new subject, addressing a new audience, and attempting to establish just the correct tone, then you can save time and write more effective documents by considering the conventions of the legal profession and by analyzing the particular needs of your audience and your purpose *before* you begin writing.

Planning complicated legal documents is rarely a simple, one-time process. In fact, you are often forced to play the *believing game* and the *doubting game*. While this suggestion may at first appear contradictory, observations of writers at work have demonstrated that you need one foot firmly planted in your role as skeptic and the other planted in your role as believer when you are unsure about how to best develop your documents. Because the writing process and legal interpretation are interrelated, your thoughts will mature, and you will make connections among ideas that at first seem unrelated. As you write, your earlier outlines may become obsolete, as indeed may your original thoughts about interpreting the law.

The Three Basic Factors in the Communication Situation

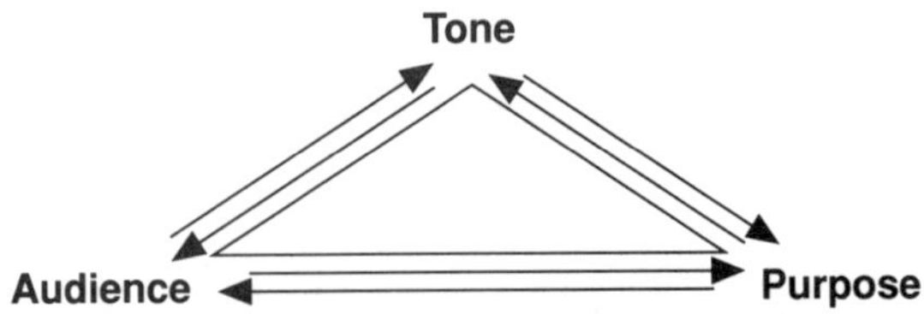

Analyzing Your Communication Situation

Every document you write—as well as *how* you write—is shaped in response to a *communication situation*. Three basic considerations determine what you say and how you say it: purpose, audience, tone. As suggested by the diagram above, changes in your audience require adjustments in your tone, as do changes in your purpose.

A communication situation for the writer is the equivalent of the gavel to the judge: you exert control over other people and ensure readability by considering your purpose for writing, the audience for the document, and the appropriate tone in light of your audience and purpose. Below is a more detailed discussion of how you can evaluate your communication situation when planning documents or oral arguments.

PURPOSE ANALYSIS

Until you know your primary purpose for writing, you cannot know what information to leave in, what to leave out, or even how to best organize a document. Of course, most legal documents are shaped by multiple purposes. A persuasive letter to an opposing attorney, for example, may have paragraphs that are intended to inform, paragraphs that are threatening, and paragraphs that request information, as well as paragraphs that persuade. However, on a more global level, every text should have one primary purpose. The purpose for most legal documents falls into one of the following categories: informative writing (memoranda), investigative writing (letters), analytical writing (opinions, memoranda), persuasive writing (briefs, memoranda, letters).

When determining the primary purpose for a document, question how the writing task relates to the matter as a whole. For example, your "updating" letter to a client does more than provide information about the current status of a case: it also clarifies your point of view about a case, impresses your client with your assiduity, and builds a record of timely correspondence with your client. All of these complementary and sometimes conflicting goals may be present when you sit down to write.

Because of the generative nature of language, your sense of the primary purpose for a document will often become clearer once you have written a few drafts. Yet because the effectiveness of a document is chiefly determined by how well you focus on addressing a primary purpose, you can save time by identifying your purpose as early as possible. Try asking the following questions when you are unsure about the purpose for a document:

1. Am I attempting to report facts objectively, to analyze legal issues, or to be persuasive?
2. Do I have competing or conflicting purposes for writing this document? If so, should the document be separated into two different documents or should it be divided into distinct parts with different headings and subheadings?
3. Am I keeping my long-term goals in perspective when addressing this document? How does this document fit into the conduct of the matter as a whole?
4. What crucial information do I need to emphasize to educate or persuade my audience? How can I organize the document to emphasize key information?

AUDIENCE ANALYSIS

To be successful, your documents must communicate information to readers in ways that account for their concerns and opinions. For example, a legal opinion that concentrates on the intricacies of the law at the expense of any concern for what the audience needs to know or what will affect the audience will be an unread or unconvincing opinion. Also, you would write about one calamity—such as a little girl being disabled by being run over by a school bus—in different ways depending on whether you are writing for lawyers and partners in your firm, clients, judges, or opposing lawyers. As you can readily conclude, what you would write in a letter to the judge is quite different from what you would write to the mother of the disabled child, although the prewriting, drafting, and revising strategies would be similar.

When beginning a writing task, you may tend to ignore your audience and focus on identifying the legal issues involved. First, of course, you may need to make sense of the issues and the scope of the case for yourself. In your notes to yourself, you should feel free to record the results of your research and your own thoughts in a haphazard way, without organizing them for a reader. A writer's first reader, as the saying goes, is always the self.

However, if your document is to be successful, you must at some point escape your own perspective and read your document from the perspective of your intended audience and critics. You can improve the quality of your writing, as well as reduce the amount of time it takes to write, by analyzing your audience when you first begin a writing project. By considering the following questions, you can determine what information you need to provide and what information you can assume that your readers know:

1. Who are the people in my audience? (Include in your answer everyone on the distribution list.)
2. What assumptions can I make about my audience's knowledge of the subject matter? What information can I assume that the audience is already aware of?
3. Is it possible that my material has multiple audiences? For example, might my letter to a client also be read by an insurance company or by another lawyer?
4. How knowledgeable are my primary and secondary audiences about the legal issues that are involved? (Remember, other lawyers without your specialization may be unfamiliar with the pertinent law.) What concepts or terms will I need to define for my audience to understand my message?
5. What attitudes about the matter can I presume my audience has? In what ways is my audience biased? Is my audience friendly or hostile? Am I writing to someone who seems fairly intelligent and reasonable? Am I addressing someone who is overcome by grief or emotional problems?
6. What level of education does my audience have? Am I writing to laypeople who dislike legal language? Will my audience be swayed or will it be insulted by emotional appeals?
7. Should I have separate sections in the document to account for the different needs of the specific audiences that I am addressing?
8. What is the political situation in which this message will be read? What provisions do I need to make to account for this situation?

TONE ANALYSIS

The challenge of juggling numerous, seemingly unrelated ideas can be so great that you may overlook the *tone* of your document. Yet, readers are looking between the lines of your documents, searching for clues about who you are and how you feel about a subject. Even when you avoid use of the first person and personal references, readers make judgments, rightly or wrongly, about what kind of person you are and about your professional abilities. All aspects of your text give clues to the reader about your personality and professional ability. Your word choice, examples, organization, sentence structure—even how you format your material—all of these textual features contribute to the tone of a document. No matter how well you fine-tune the substance of your document, the tone that readers infer significantly influences how the message is perceived. If the readers dislike the way you are presenting an argument, they may reject your presentation of the facts. No matter how solid your evidence is for a particular claim, you may not be successful if your readers think you sound sarcastic or condescending. If you do not sound confident, your readers will doubt you. Even simple spelling errors can make you look foolish.

The term *persona* refers to occasions when you disguise your natural voice and attempt to sound like someone else. For example, when negotiating a settlement, you may want to appear tired and beaten when you are truly biting your lip with joy. If you were writing a persuasive letter to an opposing lawyer, you might wish to adopt a stern, conservative, heavy-hitting persona.

As a lawyer, you generally want to present yourself as rational and objective. You will sometimes need to hide your bias and avoid appeals to emotions. To help keep the spotlight on the information that is being presented, you will typically want to "disappear" from the page as much as possible. Generally speaking, the more technical the subject, the less present is the authorial "I." For some documents, the first person may be appropriate, but always question whether the use of the first person is accepted by your audience and if it is helping to create an effective tone. (See chapter 16 for a fuller discussion of when to use the first person.)

To help you establish the appropriate tone for a communication situation before writing, ask the following questions:

1. What inferences about my personality do I want readers to make about me as an author? Do I wish to speak with the voice of a benevolent advisor or a menacing adversary? When reading my letters, will clients perceive me to be an articulate spokesperson who understands their problems? Do I appear hostile or reasonable? Have I projected a pleading tone?
2. Have I used a precise vocabulary so that the opposing counsel will perceive me and my case as formidable? Do I use any emotionally charged words that are unnecessary?

Analyzing Legal Writing Conventions

Your writing must conform to the conventions of the legal profession and your local bar. It is not uncommon, for example, for courts to limit the length of documents and prescribe the formatting features, including what titles, headings, and subheadings should be used. Therefore, ask the following questions before writing a draft:

1. What conventions exist for the kind of writing that you are doing? For example, when writing a brief have you met the requirements of the court and the customs of the local bar? Have you met the standards of your own firm?
2. If you are using a "boilerplate" (standard existing document), is it up to date? Has it been revised recently? (*Note:* There is no "rule of thumb" to determine whether boilerplate is up to date. If the law has changed, so must the boilerplate. Some boilerplate must change every year. If in doubt, do not use it.)

Analyzing Practical Constraints on the Writing Task

Each time you begin a document, weigh the importance of the project against your other responsibilities. To determine how much time you can allocate to it, question how your partners and associates would evaluate its significance. The familiar phrase "time is of the essence" is never more true than in the practice of law.

When you first begin drafting legal documents, you may need an inordinate amount of time. This can be particularly true if you lack extensive writing experience. Unfortunately, there is no substitute for a "baptism by fire." We can only become more effective at writing by writing regularly and experimenting with the various prewriting, revising, and editing strategies discussed in this book. If you are relatively inexperienced as a writer, you must find solace in the assumption that eventually you will need less time to write and revise documents.

However, if you are a perfectionist, you may always have trouble completing documents. Remember, a piece of writing is seldom perfect. And the economics of your practice require that you keep your perfectionist expectations in check. Asking the following questions can help you do this:

1. Whose interests not a party to the document may be affected?
2. How much time can you bill for the particular matter you are working on? (Do not, for example, spend three hours drafting a $200 collection letter.)
3. What is your relationship to your client?

Establishing Reasonable Writing Goals

Perhaps in college you had the luxury to set aside several days and weekends to complete a long writing project. However, your hectic schedule may now prevent you from having large blocks of time in which you can go on a writing binge. Instead of putting the work off till you have a chunk of time available to really concentrate, you must learn to use short blocks of time. If you prefer to binge, you may have some difficulty establishing a regular writing schedule. Yet little is more important to your development as a writer than regular writing.

The writing required by a multimillion dollar case may weigh hundreds of pounds and may require several years of preparation. At the advent of the case, the prospect of writing all of these pages can be intimidating. If you procrastinate and focus on the big picture, the immensity of the writing task can be overwhelming. Like a New Year's resolution that seems so impossible to achieve that you might as well forget it, you can actually handicap your ability to write if you just think about the due date and the numerous pages that must be written. However, if you break each task down into parts, you will realize that you can easily manage the work load. As the novelist Margaret Atwood once wisely pointed out, anyone can write a novel once he or she realizes that a page a day for a year will suffice.

If you are bored by a project or prone to procrastinate, you may want to keep a daily record of work achieved, number of words written, number of words revised, and goals for revising the text. By logging your work in this manner, you will develop a more realistic sense of how much time you need to set aside for writing. Asking the following questions can also help you schedule your time in a productive manner:

1. If the document is likely to be a long one, what major sections can be written according to a realistic schedule?
2. How much time do you have to draft the document?
3. What realistic due dates can you establish for a nearly final or final draft?

Talking with Colleagues About the Legal Matter

No one in your firm will care about your writing as much as you do. Other associates or partners simply do not have the time to carefully critique your manuscripts. However, once you have polished your documents to the best of your ability, you should solicit and heed your colleagues' criticisms.

Although your classmates from law school and the members of your firm have their own cases and deadlines to meet, most lawyers are willing to exchange ideas, to talk about difficult cases, to analyze difficult concepts. Cultivate the habit of talking to other lawyers whenever you can and encourage others to approach you. It is really quite amazing how another lawyer can look briefly at a problem that you have agonized over and quickly suggest a new avenue of approach.

Final Comments

At some point, time spent prewriting becomes procrastination. Evaluating your intended audience, voice, and purpose; taking notes or conducting more research; talking over your ideas with colleagues or drawing tentative outlines—these sorts of activities can quickly become counterproductive if taken to the extreme. Eventually you need to take the plunge and begin drafting.

CHAPTER 2

Drafting: Harnessing the Generative Nature of Language

As a lawyer, you are highly skilled at analysis and criticism. Your legal training has provided you with the ability to look beyond the emotional aspects of issues and to analyze the underlying structure of arguments. While essential, your training as a skeptic can handicap you when it comes to starting a writing project. Many lawyers are so skilled at criticizing ideas that they are too quick to shoot down their own insights.

In this chapter, we show you numerous ways to avoid procrastinating and begin the drafting process. While in the previous chapter we encouraged you to play both the *believing game* and the *doubting game*, we now ask that you solely play the *believing game*. By placing trust in your intuitive self and the generative nature of language, you will be able to avoid worrying about your writing load and get the work done in a quick and efficient manner. The strategies for developing and organizing your ideas discussed in this chapter provide a healthy alternative to attempting to writing perfect first drafts.

Drafting Strategies: Developing Your Ideas

Instead of attempting to compose a perfect first draft or agonizing over each sentence, try to be flexible about your plans and to generate as much material possible. If new ideas occur to you when writing, do not quickly dismiss them even if they seem unrelated. We make this suggestion because research has indicated that the thinking process often works inductively—that is, you begin with numerous specifics and slowly move toward a general conclusion or "aha!" insight. Often you cannot write the introduction to a document, which establishes the focus and organization of the document, until you have stumbled around some and written a few drafts.

FREEWRITING

Freewriting is a deceptively simple, yet extraordinary powerful, activity. Simply put, to freewrite is to write as quickly as possible without stopping. Because your hands can tire from writing or typing without stopping, you may want to limit freewriting sessions to ten to fifteen minute intervals.

Freewriting can be distinguished from more traditional approaches to drafting in several ways. First, freewriting involves ignoring critical questions and self-doubt. When you are unsure about how to spell a word, do not stop to look it up in a dictionary. Do not stop writing even if you are unsure about what you should say next. Instead, write, " I can't think of what to say next." After you repeat this phrase several times, your mind will discover something to say. Occasionally the products of your freewriting will net little, yet other times the force of your effort will trigger an original insight. Second, freewriting allows you to be more selective about which sentences and paragraphs are worth keeping. When rereading the results of your freewriting, highlight or circle passages that go to the heart of what you hope to express. Third, freewriting can be an invaluable way to unleash the vigorous voice that characterizes effective prose. When you do a lot of stopping and starting, your prose can sound choppy, forced. When you are summarizing extensive legal research, the material that you have researched and the order in which you discovered the information can quickly overtake the voice you are attempting to develop. However, when you let your thoughts about the research flow, your language often gains forcefulness, a sense of directness, that you otherwise might have difficulty achieving. Eventually—particularly when you are deeply involved in a particular case—you will be able to use substantial chunks from your freewriting as solid drafts that require little revision.

When mining your freewriting products for useful ideas, place brackets [ ] around passages that seem worth keeping. Cross out passages that should be deleted. Highlight ideas that keep popping up. If they do not appear related to your subject, copy them down on a separate sheet of paper or place them in a separate document file on your computer because they may be surprisingly useful later on. At this early stage, you do not want to censor your thinking. To identify the dominant purpose that unites the freewritten passage, summarize in a sentence the substance of what you have written and then take that sentence, record it on a separate sheet of paper or in a separate document, and use it to begin a second freewrite. By looping from one freewriting passage to another, you can quickly generate a thousand words instead of struggling to write 300 words.

Freewriting can be unnecessary if you immediately know the gist of a message and how it should be delivered. Yet when confronting complicated legal issues, when no simple solutions exist, we need to think deeply about our subjects. And rather than trusting our minds to work out the problem, we can save time by putting ideas down on the page and then letting thoughts collect and contradict each other. Soon we can sort out what emotional appeals and logical appeals we can best make for a particular audience.

At first, freewriting may seem silly and wasteful. In ten minutes, for instance, you can generate 500 words or more, and it may seem wasteful to throw away 450 of those words. Yet consider the problems with more traditional ways of writing: when you try to write a sophisticated argument or analysis in several drafts, your preliminary thoughts can tyrannize later drafts. After all, when you invest time in carefully selecting and positioning words, you will feel committed to these words—even if fresh insights challenge you to reconsider what you have said or how you have organized your material.

When you first attempt freewriting, it may appear chaotic, forced, and unnatural. You will probably have to fight the urge to reread phrases or check passages against sources. Yet after practicing this strategy for a while, you will soon find that it allows you to shatter writing blocks and to write more effective legal documents.

USE FILE DOCUMENTS AS A POINT OF DEPARTURE

Because the economics of the practice of law prohibit wasted time, most firms maintain a library of standard documents for various purposes, such as wills, contracts, and pleadings. You should avoid the temptation of relying extensively on these kinds of boilerplate. Often the labor involved in finding appropriate boilerplate and then transforming it for your audience and purpose exceeds the effort involved in writing a quick first draft.

When severely pressed for time, however, you may want to use these forms, while ensuring, of course, that you have changed the names of parties. We strongly recommend, however, that you treat these only as a first draft; use them as you would a first draft you have drawn up yourself, and then revise them so that the document accurately reflects the needs of your particular case. Do not fall into the trap of using a document—although it may be similar in purpose to yours—that was written for a different audience, about a different set of facts, and in someone else's language. Use old documents to *cue* your thinking, not to *constrain* it, or shape it.

DICTATE DRAFTS

Dictating your ideas and notes can be a surprisingly productive way to begin drafting even complicated legal documents. By keeping your dictating machine nearby, you can quickly record insights that occur to you about project A when you are working on project C. Be receptive to good ideas whenever they come to you and keep a minirecorder in your briefcase so you can record insights as they occur. If you are maneuvering through traffic on your way to work and an idea hits you, be sure to record it then (but avoid hitting another lawyer on his or her way to work).

ASK THE JOURNALISTS' QUESTIONS

To avoid overlooking important material, reporters often ask the *Journalists' 5Ws: Who?, What?, Where?, When?, Why?*, and *How?* When you are narrating events that led up to a significant event, you may find it useful to consider how these questions apply to your particular case. For example, in setting out the facts of a breach of contract case, do you have all of the names of the involved parties? Are the events in chronological order? Are the dates correct?

Drafting Strategies: Organizing Your Ideas

When your readers set your document down, shrug their shoulders, and say, "So what?" you know your organization or development of content has failed you. Unfortunately, poor organization is not a rarity. Many legal documents are impenetrable because they are weighted down by unconnected facts. For example, when you are writing a brief, you can understandably become so bogged down in a thorough review of the law that you fail to explain how the law applies to the facts of a case. Likewise, your desire to adequately describe the unique facts of the case can intrude on your ability to adequately express how these facts relate to the law. It is equally possible to review the law and the facts of the case yet still not clarify how the facts and law relate to each other.

If your documents are poorly organized, you will lack credibility. In time, you may also lack clients. All of the hours you spent researching the problem are in vain when you fail to establish a coherent and emphatic organization. Other lawyers, judges, and clients simply do not have the time to filter through what you have written and infer your message or its significance.

Legal writing textbooks invariably admonish lawyers to produce a complete outline of a manuscript before writing. This recommendation is based on the assumption that thinking and writing are not related: that first you think and then you write. Minutes spent outlining your work, textbook authors frequently claim, can save you hours in the drafting process. Now while this advice is certainly well intended, it has a few drawbacks. First, when addressing a complex legal situation, you will sometimes be unable to write an outline for your document until you have written a few drafts. You may very well not know what claims to make or what issues should be defined until you have struggled to express a legal problem. If you have ever started to write an answer to a law school or bar examination question and then had to strike it and start over, you will understand what we mean. Second, you need to consider organization to be an ongoing process. Rather than organizing your presentation once and then proceeding to hammer home the pertinent points, you will often need to reconsider your original intentions and organization once you have written a few drafts. When new information becomes available or you have a new insight about the issues or facts of law, you may need to reorganize the outline. Third, rigid rules about writing must be rejected. For whatever reason, although some people work best from outlines, others cannot work with them, so they need other approaches to help structure their documents.

Establishing the context of the problem, clarifying your purpose, forecasting your organization, providing a coherent and thorough discussion of each issue, elaborating on how the law applies to the facts, drawing dynamic, forceful conclusions—these are important goals when organizing your work. However, you often will not be able to accomplish these goals until you have written a few drafts.

Rather than suggesting that you should first organize your ideas and then write, we recommend that you outline your documents *before* you write, *while* you write, and *after* you have written. However, you need not necessarily begin with a formal outline. Instead, as we describe below, you may wish to first cluster your ideas and then place them in a pie diagram or an issue tree. As your thinking matures with each subsequent draft, you can revise your outline to account for your increased control over the subject matter.

DRAW A CLUSTER DIAGRAM

When you are beginning a new case, you may be unsure about the logical relationships between your ideas, about what rules should be applied, or about what information needs to be stressed. Rather than try to force your ideas into a formal outline, you can pictorially represent them on the page and then draw lines between ideas that seem somewhat related. The following sample cluster diagram shows the result of recording and relating ideas on a topic.

Sample Cluster Diagram

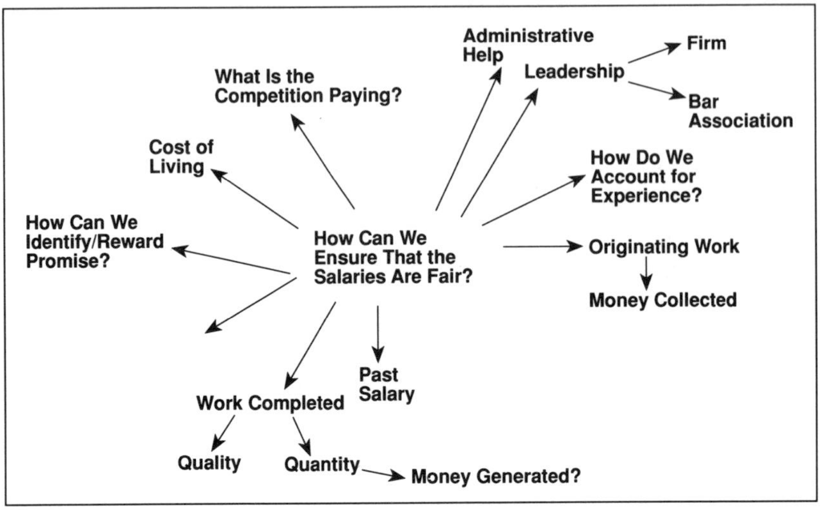

DRAW A PIE DIAGRAM

Once you have produced a cluster diagram and identified basic topics, you can draw a pie diagram that illustrates the basic points in your analysis. Pie diagrams allow you to visually estimate how much time you will spend addressing each aspect of your subject. If you believe, for example, that issue A deserves a more involved discussion than issues B through E, you can draw it as a bigger piece of the pie. You will find this especially useful when there are restraints applicable either to time allotted or length of document permitted.

DRAW AN ISSUE TREE

When you do have a sense of how events relate to each other and you can put them in a narrative structure or show cause-and-effect relationships, then you can best illustrate these relationships by drawing an *issue tree*. As with cluster diagrams, issue trees allow you to pictorially represent your thinking. However, rather than drawing them in a random, disorganized fashion, you can impose an order on your ideas by placing them in *tree form*. This will help you define the primary issues and their attendant subissues. If you find yourself unable to connect an idea to some part of the diagram, then you should review your purpose for writing the document and decide whether the tangential information should be placed in your document.

The primary advantage of drawing an issue tree instead of writing a formal outline is that it helps you see how your ideas are connected

Sample Pie Diagram

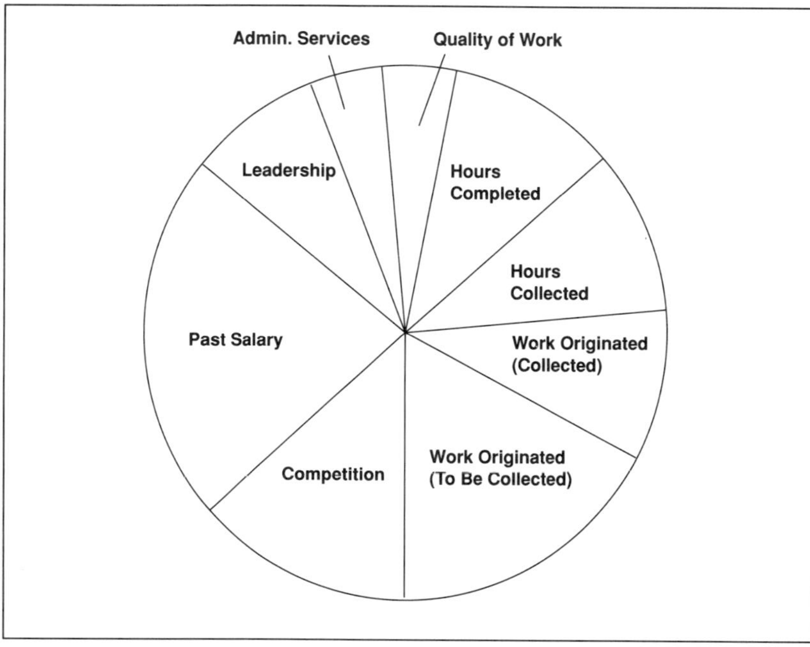

Sample Issue Tree

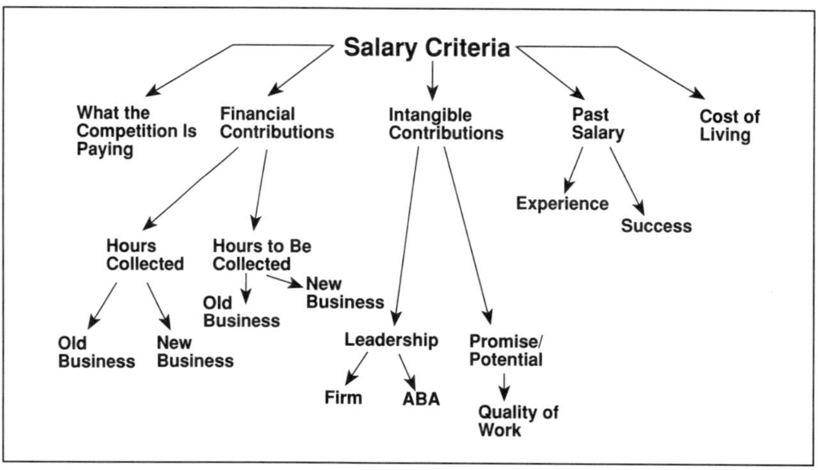

and whether or not certain ideas are connected to the main arguments. When ideas do not connect with earlier ideas, you will be more likely to see this problem when you draw your ideas in an issue tree form than cast them in the more linear form of an outline.

OUTLINE TENTATIVE PLANS

Writing outlines is probably one of the most frequently mentioned organizational techniques. The advantage of a well-constructed outline is that it may help you identify gaps in your reasoning and presentation. While it may be counterproductive, even impossible, to draft an outline when first beginning a project, we strongly recommend drafting an informal, tentative outline once.

Sample Formal Outline

Purpose Statement: In one sentence, summarize the purpose of your document. For example, "We need to account for the financial contributions, the intangible contributions, and past salaries of associates and partners when determining salary increases."

I. *Major Theme Related to Purpose:*
   Financial Contributions

   A. Hours collected
      1. Old business
      2. New business

   B. Hours to be collected
      1. Old business
      2. New business

II. *Major Theme Related to Purpose:*
   Intangible Contributions

   1. Leadership
      a. To firm
      b. To ABA
   2. Promise/potential
      a. As perceived by colleagues
      b. As perceived by clients
      c. As perceived by competitors

III. *Major Theme Related to Purpose: Past Salary*

   1. Experience
   2. Success

Final Comments

This chapter presented some suggestions for how to develop ideas as you begin to draft a document. The organizing strategies discussed in this chapter provide flexible ways to gain control over whole documents. If you have more specific questions about the conventions for organizing documents, conclusions, or the body of persuasive and expository documents, you can refer to the chapters in Part III.

PART II

The Unified Case Study Approach: Preparing Basic Legal Documents

CHAPTER 3

Pulling the Case Together: Writing the File Memorandum

For the next seven chapters, we ask that you play the role of an attorney in a fictitious case, which we will call *Ames v. The Brinkman School for the Impaired* (or simply "the Ames case"). By analyzing the various writing demands that this case would place on you as the plaintiff's lawyer (and in chapters 6 and 9 as the lawyer for the insurance company), we analyze how to write effective legal documents, such as memoranda for the file, letters to clients, and trial briefs.

Getting the Facts: Interviewing

When you interview clients, keep in mind that they may fail to tell you everything they know about the case. Sometimes clients neglect to report the facts to their attorneys because they think the omitted facts are not important, and sometimes a client's emotional state makes a full exploration of the facts impossible at the first meeting. Of course, the initial interview may elicit all the useful information the client has, but more often you will need to think about the case and complete some preliminary research before identifying all the legal implications the case presents. Thus, you may often require a second interview, usually by telephone, to elicit further facts. Since you often begin a case with your interview of the client or his or her representative, we will briefly explain how you can best get the information you need from interviews.

DEVELOP AN INTERVIEWING STRATEGY

The limited amount of time available to you for interviewing dictates that you use time efficiently. Whenever possible, you should prepare your questions in advance. You already have most of the skill required to be an effective interviewer: as a social human being you have a sensitivity to how people open up to questions or clam up. And while you should naturally rely on your innate people skills, as a lawyer you also need to develop a strategy to ensure that you get the information you need quickly and efficiently.

By using the term "strategy," we do not mean to imply that you should attempt to manipulate interviewees and try to force a particular outcome. Indeed, effective interviewers set their biases aside and learn to listen attentively during interviews so that the interviewees can feel free to express themselves. The successful interviewer masks any impatience and, as much as time will allow, lets the interviewee do the talking.

When we suggest that you need a "strategy," we mean that you should ensure that the environment for the interview is conducive to sharing information, that you have a clear focus about why you are conducting the interview, that you have devised appropriate questions to solicit the desired information, and that you are sufficiently flexible to respond to new issues as they develop during the interview.

Often the interviewee is not obliged to meet with you, and you may even be an unwelcome interruption in his or her day, so you will need to be flexible about where and for how long you meet and whether or not it is acceptable for you to tape-record the session. In general, you should try to get the interviewee away from as many distractions as possible. Establishing a climate of trust and support is difficult when the interviewee is bombarded with phone calls, piles of messages, lists of things to do, and colleagues and secretaries running in and out with questions.

Be aware that many of us have the tendency to tighten up and withhold information when we sense that we are speaking for the record. Therefore, you need to be calm and relaxed; remember that your body language invariably sends messages about whether you are bored or frustrated or in disagreement with the interviewee's comments. Rather than being quick to judge the interviewee's comments and their usefulness to you, try to focus on being a receptive listener. Show tact in your responses and carefully interject humor to put the interviewee at ease.

If the interviewee does not mind having the session taped, then you would be wise to pretest your recorder and ensure that the batteries are fresh. Incidentally, some interviewers use two recorders to avoid the embarrassment of discovering too late that the recorder did not work. A second useful tip is to use microrecorders, that is, small recorders that use minicassettes. Finally, try to place the recorder out of the interviewee's eyesight and avoid looking at it, discussing it, or checking to see whether or not it is working so that it is forgotten as soon as possible. If the interviewee appears distracted by the recorder even though he or she has not objected, you would be wise to remove it and take careful notes instead.

You do not want to appear rigid when interviewing any witness or your client, so be careful not to fire questions at an interviewee in an adversarial fashion. Instead, you should try to couch your questions in a more relaxed, discussion-format style. Asking spontaneous questions—questions that occur to you in response to the interviewee's comments—allows you to demonstrate that you are paying close attention to what the interviewee has to say. During your first interview with your client, you will probably have no choice but to ask spontaneous questions, unless you have background information from the client, either from a letter or from your initial phone conversation in which the appointment was set up. In such cases, you will want to spend at least a few minutes before the interview drawing up a list of questions and have it in front of you when you begin the interview.

REVIEWING THE FIRST INTERVIEW

Let us now suppose that you have met with your client Mr. Ames on April 29 and have so far developed these facts:

> Mr. John Henry Ames is a widower who resides with his eight-year-old daughter, Susan, at his home in Tampa, Florida. Because Susan was born deaf, she attends a special school, the Brinkman School for the Impaired (BSI), for children with hearing and psychological impairments and deficiencies. On school days, Susan is picked up in front of her home by the school's bus, Busarus, at about 6:50 A.M. and delivered to the school with eight to ten other children on the same bus route. On the date of the accident, Susan was struck by the bus after it had dropped the students off and as it was leaving the school. Susan was taken to the emergency room of the nearest hospital where she was treated for multiple injuries.

The remaining facts of the case are set forth in appendix I, where you will find a newspaper report of the injury to Susan and a police report with witnesses' statements attached. All of this information should be deposited in the case file for your possible future use and for any other member of your firm who wishes to read the original documents.

The Nature of a File Memorandum

You will want to open a case file after the first meeting with your client and put a comprehensive office memorandum into it in addition to the various documents. The purpose of this memorandum is to inform other members of your firm about the case and to enable you to keep track of the case yourself. As additional facts are gathered from various sources, and as your research clarifies (or at least exposes) the legal issues raised by the facts, you will want to prepare additional office memoranda. Not only does the initial file memorandum serve as a memory refresher and summary, it also has strategic value. The file memorandum is the first document you will usually prepare in a case, and it is written after the first meeting with the client. Its purpose is to make a record of the preliminary facts of the case you have learned from the client (and from any relevant papers the client may have brought with him or her), to identify for further study the issues these facts raise, and to list additional facts that must be learned. And, as you know, additional facts may lead to new issues, and so on.

Although the primary purpose of the file memorandum is to make a descriptive record of facts and ideas, this memorandum also allows you to set down reminders to yourself regarding facts that must be developed or discovered and issues that need to be researched. Thus, it is not only a record, but also a way of learning about the case—an opportunity for you to think on paper. This clearly does not mean that you will set down your ideas in the final draft of the memorandum just as they have occurred to you. It does mean, however, that you can use the writing process as a means of clarifying your own thinking so that the final draft of the memorandum that goes into the file and that is circulated to interested partners represents a clear picture of the client's needs and the work the lawyers representing him or her need to do.

Eventually, the series of office memoranda that will be generated during the conduct of the case will present a complete statement of the facts and the issues of law, including strengths and weaknesses of both the plaintiff's and the defendant's cases. From this series of memoranda, any lawyer picking up the file can, after appropriate study, generate complete and accurate pleadings, motions, and trial briefs. It will of course also serve you as a valuable record of how the case developed and how your own thinking evolved. You will learn a great deal about trial preparation simply from writing file memoranda.

Identifying the Communication Situation

As with any writing task, you can most efficiently manage your time by analyzing the elements of the communication situation. This simply means having a clear picture of what you want to say, why you want to say it, to whom you are saying it, and how you want to say it. In short, you need to understand purpose, audience, and tone. When drafting a file memorandum, you should recognize, for instance, that your potential audience (of course, everyone who has access to the memorandum will not necessarily read it) consists of other partners who may be concerned with the conduct of the case. Your purpose is to collect the facts and analyze the issues. The memorandum must not only be complete and accurate, but also its style must reflect that you, as a competent lawyer, are both a clear thinker and a proficient writer.

Keep in mind that this memorandum is not, unlike a trial memorandum or brief, intended to persuade; you should be as objective as possible. Thus, you must be careful to omit from your report all of the emotional baggage that the client carried with him or her. Also, disclose all of the gaps in your case that must be filled in with additional work, including those that may turn out unfavorable to your case. Neither your client nor your partners will be grateful for a cosmetic treatment of the truth as you see it.

Strategies for Writing a First Draft

1. Dictate or freewrite the facts in no particular order, making sure only to get all of them from all of the sources that are presently available. At this point, you should not speculate on what facts may appear upon further investigation; rather you should stick to what is known.
2. Organize the facts into chronological order. When you have insights about interpreting the data or about the legal questions involved, you may wish to jot them down on a separate sheet of paper or in a separate document file. However, in the memo to the file, you should make no effort to emphasize any facts or speculate about them; simply get them down in an organized manner.
3. Consider the legal issues that are raised. During this preliminary stage, you should not expect to develop a full-scale argument, but you do want to identify the significant issues raised by the case. You will, of course, find *Corpus Juris Secundum* and other general encyclopedic reference works useful at this stage. Yet you should save the precedents and interpretations for later

when you are writing an internal memo in preparation for trial, as we will discuss in chapter 5. At this early point in your composing, you may find freewriting to be a particularly useful way to think about the legal issues because when you are writing you are also giving your thoughts a focus. (Please see chapter 2 for ideas on how to begin drafting and how to organize your materials.) Freewriting involves writing down ideas as they occur to you without attempting to put them in any particular order and without doing anything that might impede the flow of ideas. By reading what you have written down in the course of freewriting, you will find the basic materials that you can use in developing your draft.

4. Review your facts again. Consider what additional facts will be needed to explore fully the legal issues, and get these down in outline form. Examining the legal rules applicable to the case, as you have done in the preceding step, will suggest what facts are necessary to make a successful case of negligence or gross negligence. One of the most important things you will do in the conduct of this case is comparing the required facts with the facts you have, and noting the difference. Later, of course, you will make more subtle distinctions in interpreting the ruling case law applicable to your case as you prepare the internal memo.

Conventions for a File Memorandum

You are now ready to begin to write a first draft. Follow the format outlined on the following pages unless your firm has established a format which differs from ours.

Revising and Copyediting Your Memorandum

After you have a first draft of your memorandum, you can begin revising your work. To do so, turn to the chapters on revising and copyediting documents in Part IV. These are chapters 15, 16, and 17. The suggestions in those chapters apply to all the legal documents you prepare in this part of the book.

Use the checklist on page 35 as you review the substance of your file memorandum.

Format for a File Memorandum

To: File
From: Your Name
Re: Ames, plaintiff v. The Brinkman School for the Impaired, and School Insurance and Surety Corp., defendants.
Date: April 30, 1992
File: A92X27

Statement of Facts

You may wish to begin by stating which party your firm represents and what the relationship is. For example, if Ames is the president of a corporate client, indicate this. All of the facts of the Ames case known so far must be set out in a readable narrative. Generally, you will find it easiest to do so if you follow this plan:

1. First, set out the facts known about Mr. Ames and Susan. Obviously, you will want to mention that Susan is deaf and attends a special school.
2. Next, set out the facts known about the accident in chronological order.
3. Provide a summary of the documentary and testimonial evidence. Indicate your sources. At this point do not editorialize about the veracity of witnesses by comments such as "Obviously, the teacher is biased and may be hiding something." Save that for the courtroom (if the case gets that far).
4. Provide a summary (brief and to the point) of the medical evidence. Do not attempt to interpret the medical evidence. Confine yourself to reducing it to as few words as possible, using the doctors' language where absolutely necessary.

Issues Presented

Indicate the relevant legal rule for each issue.

Discussion

This section represents the most critical part of a lawyer's work. In it, you will raise doubts and questions, and you will indicate the additional legal research and factual material that is required. This section and the *Recommended Action* section, which follows, are most important, since they communicate your analysis and evaluation of the case. For example, it is obvious that the issues of negligence and perhaps strict liability are raised in the Ames case. Therefore, you may wish to introduce the following entry from *CJS:*

Format for a File Memorandum (continued)

> Gross negligence is materially greater than ordinary negligence, and consists of an entire absence of even slight care or diligence. (65 *CJS* 8(4); see also note 45 citing two Florida cases)

However, for any excerpts from *CJS* to be meaningful, you must relate them to the facts. One obvious place for additional research is the Florida Statutes, and *Florida Jur 2d.* You would find that 38 *Florida Jur 2d* 51 discusses strict liability under statutes designed to protect "a particular class of persons." (Is Susan Ames a member of such a class of persons?) Proceeding in this way in your file memorandum on the Ames case, you will have provided a succinct summary of the law.

Recommended Actions

Indicate what immediate actions need to be taken. What research is required? What investigative reports and other documents are needed? Where can you go for needed information? For example, you might suggest the necessity of obtaining the contract between BSI, the school in the case, and the operator of the bus, a Florida corporation known as Busarus.

You may wish to determine what licenses are required to operate a school bus in the state of Florida and the city of Tampa. Also, you may wish to consider naming the bus company as a defendant and putting it and its insurance company on notice now. Some of the same considerations will apply to the driver of the bus. You may wish to determine which of the potential defendants is in fact insured and by whom in order to evaluate what your chances of collection for an ultimate judgment might be. You may also wish to consider the possibility that one or more of the corporate defendants may be a not-for-profit corporation. If so, how will this fact affect your case?

As you can see from the example considerations, one idea leads to another, and your memo is not complete until you have raised all of the questions suggested by the case. You are not yet obliged, however, to answer all of these questions.

Checklist: File Memorandum

Purpose

Have you kept to the purpose of informing, not persuading? The standard purpose of a memorandum is to inform other members of the firm about the case, to serve as a record of the case, and to help you clarify your thinking on a case.

Audience

Have you presented information so that other lawyers in your firm can understand it and read it easily?

Tone

Have you kept an objective, unemotional tone?

Organization

1. Have you included these or similar sections: standard memo heading, *Statement of Facts, Issues Presented, Discussion, Recommended Actions?*
2. Have you put the facts in chronological order?
3. Have you put the recommended actions in chronological order or order of importance?
4. If this is a subsequent file memorandum, as the case is in progress, have you divided the *Facts* and *Discussion* sections to discuss the new facts and old ones?

Contents

1. Have you included all the facts that you know up to this point?
2. Have you indicated gaps in the facts that must be filled?
3. Have you identified the significant legal issues in the case?
4. If this is a subsequent file memo, as the case is in progress, have you discussed the new facts and their impact on the old facts?

CHAPTER 4

Further Developments: Subsequent File Memoranda

You have studied the format and content of a file memorandum in chapter 3. The style of subsequent memoranda will be identical to that of the initial one, except that they will provide only the new facts or summarize products of your research and analysis of any new issues raised by the new information.

Handling New Facts About a Case

Suppose that two more pieces of factual evidence have become available to you:

1. You have received the medical report from the physician at Children's Hospital who examined Susan. (See appendices II and III for the medical documents.)
2. You have received a copy of the report of the investigator who was assigned by the Children's Division of the Department of Welfare to look into the accident.

Obviously, both the physician's report and the investigator's report have significant bearing on the general issues of liability and measure of damages. The gravity of the injuries suffered by Susan, the amount of pain, the length of the recovery period, and the question of whether she will be permanently impaired or will recover completely are all factual questions that will need to be examined. After carefully reading the hospital medical report in appendix II, you should ask the following questions: Is it clear what the initial report of Susan's examination at Children's Hospital means, or does the report require clarification? What further evidence are you going to need and how are you going to get it?

The report of the "disinterested" investigator for the state is critically important. If it is favorable to your case, you will want to introduce it in evidence; if it is not, the other side will. Examine it not only for what it says but also for what it omits to say or says ambiguously. Make a note of any points that you may clarify by taking a deposition. Also, make a list of all of the facts that the investigator has introduced into the report. Next, compare the list with what you already know about the case, and then prepare a list of the new facts.

1. What facts have been ambiguously presented? What issues need clarification?
2. What new facts have been presented?
3. What contradictions exist between the new information and the information presented in the first file memorandum?

Once you have carefully studied the two reports, you should be prepared to write another file memorandum. This one will be somewhat more complicated than the first, because now you are introducing new facts on top of the old, and some of these may contradict "facts" you had previously in hand. Thus, you now have four categories of facts to consider in your memorandum, and it should be organized around these categories.

1. New facts, uncontradicted so far
2. New facts, contradicting "old" facts
3. New support for "old" facts
4. Ambiguities and possible omissions requiring further investigation

As you examine the new facts, you will want to determine whether any additional issues are raised. For example, consider this statement in the state investigator's report:

> Clearly the school staff felt the transportation procedures implemented at the school were inadequate. No written record of follow-up was available at the school for review.

This statement of the investigator raises several significant implications: First, although the "school staff" are probably not qualified to give expert opinions about the efficacy of the school's transportation services, even as nonexpert witnesses their testimony is helpful to your case. Second, and more important, this finding suggests that the teachers complained to the school's administrators about transportation problems, so we have evidence that the school authorities were on notice that they were allowing a dangerous practice. Third, note the investigator's statement that the record of follow-up was not "available." Does this mean that the school refused to provide it, that the school could not find its record of follow-up, or that there was not any such record? Each of these possibilities has different implications that you must consider.

Organizing a Subsequent File Memorandum

The best way to organize subsequent memoranda is to use the same format you used for the first memorandum. Use the same section headings, but under the heading *Statement of Facts* divide the information into the four sections we have suggested above, marking each section with a sequential number or letter for the convenience of readers who may wish to respond with questions or comments. Under *Issues Presented* and *Discussion,* follow the same setup of subdividing old and new information. Under the last section, *Recommended Actions,* however, you will not need to subdivide. Instead, *Recommended Actions* should include an expanded list of the things that need to be done, the specific action to be taken, and an explanation of how that action relates to the *Discussion* section. For example, in the *Discussion* section you will address the significance of this statement found in the state investigator's report:

> A list of recommendations made by teachers, some of which may be incorporated into a plan of correction, has been submitted to the Central Office by the principal of the school. All information clearly points out the need to address the transportation procedures and policies at the school without delay.

Obviously, the content of this list of recommendations is very significant to your case. Getting it as soon as possible must be one of your principal concerns.

You can organize the *Recommended Actions* part of the memorandum by listing the actions with their accompanying explanations and justifications either in their order of importance or in chronological order. Use chronological order only if there is a strong sequential relationship among the actions—that is, if certain things can only be done after others are done. Otherwise, you should opt for a list that addresses the most important needs first.

Suggested Format for Subsequent Memoranda

Statement of Facts

1. New facts, uncontradicted so far
2. New facts, contradicting "old" facts
3. New support for "old" facts
4. Ambiguities and possible omissions requiring further investigation

Issues Presented

1. New legal issues
2. Old legal issues in light of new facts
3. Possible further legal issues requiring additional facts

Discussion

1. New facts, uncontradicted so far
2. New facts, contradicting "old" facts
3. New support for "old" facts
4. Ambiguities and possible omissions requiring further investigation

Recommended Actions

1. How do the actions that should be taken relate to the facts as they now exist?
2. What further legal research is indicated?
3. On the issue of damages, what research is indicated?

Note that in answering the question on damages, your research is not exclusively bibliographic. Appellate courts often rule on issues of damages, but their decisions will not give you much idea of what the injuries sustained by your client's daughter are "worth" before a jury or in settlement. That will require some research either in the courthouse, looking at actual damage awards, and/or by asking questions of trial lawyers who frequently handle tort cases.

Drafting and Revising the Memorandum

Naturally, you should write the first draft of any subsequent file memoranda just as you wrote the first draft of the initial memorandum; then you subject your draft to a careful process of revising and editing. When you are certain it is "perfect," you can distribute and file it. By being single-minded in your pursuit of perfection, you will find that your memos have none or at the most only one or two mistakes each, as opposed to the dozen or more that will result from a lesser degree of care. Some of these errors will be minor, but the compound effect of a series of even minor errors or omissions will not lend you panache. On the contrary, your readers will get an impression of you as a lawyer who is not careful, not accurate, and not thorough. Outside of a reputation for unethical practice, that is the worst reputation a lawyer can get.

When you revise your file memorandum, use the checklist on page 35 to see if you have met the criteria for effective file memoranda.

In the memorandum for the Ames case, one of the *Recommended Actions* paragraphs must deal with the medical evidence you have accumulated so far. It is apparent from the original medical report written by Dr. Kenneth Jones that Susan Ames has suffered some rather severe injuries. Note that she was transferred to the pediatric intensive care unit. Since this medical testimony about the injuries to Susan Ames is critically important to your case, one of the recommended actions that will be very high on your list is likely to be an interview with Dr. Jones and any other physicians who examined her.

It is still too early to take depositions. You are not yet certain of the legal issues in the case, but you will certainly want to clarify any language in the medical report that is either ambiguous or too technical for the layperson to understand. Note also that the doctor reports that the van was moving approximately twenty miles per hour. How does the doctor know this? Note that in the medical report under *Follow-up*, Dr. Jones recommends that Dr. Smith of Orthopedic should see the patient "in one week for evaluation of her extremity fractures." You may wish to make a note about this in the file for follow-up on the issue of damages.

Writing a Short Supplementary Memorandum

Suppose that about two weeks after you have written the second memorandum, you receive two additional important pieces of information: two letters from doctors. (You will find the letters in appendix III.) One of them is a letter from a professor of plastic surgery at Children's Hospital Medical Center. The professor states that he examined Susan Ames and that she sustained severe lacerations to her legs. He recommends plastic surgery to relieve the scarring. The other letter is from a doctor of pediatric ophthalmology, who writes that Susan has developed "bilateral sixth nerve-end palsy as a consequence of head trauma." This doctor explains that damage to the sixth nerve caused a palsy that resulted in crossed eyes. In order to restore normal vision, the doctor indicates the necessity of operating on the eye muscles. Obviously, these two letters bear importantly on the issue of damages. Both of them suggest surgery, and in both cases—especially in the case of the medical surgery to correct the scars—100% recovery is not predicted. Note that Dr. Miller, the professor of plastic surgery, indicates the patient "will always have residual scar tissue in these areas." Although as a matter of law the severity of the injuries bears only on damages, you will of course immediately recognize that Susan, who is already deaf, will now be additionally handicapped, a fact that is bound to affect a jury emotionally.

At this point, you will of course want to write an additional file memorandum. However, since these two new pieces of information bear only on the issue of damages, rather than on the issue of liability, you will not need to write a complete new memorandum. You can follow the same format that you have used before, indicate that you are supplying additional information bearing on the issue of damages, and make reference to the two letters, which you will place in the file. Obviously, in the *Recommended Actions* section of the memorandum, you will want to recommend at the very least interviews with the two doctors to clarify and expand on the information, so that when depositions are taken later, you will know what questions you want to ask. More important, in the *Discussion* section of the memorandum, you may wish to note that this is beginning to shape up as a case that the defendants, including the insurance company, may not want to bring to trial.

CHAPTER 5

Shaping the Case: Writing an Internal Memo

At this point in your conduct of the Ames case, it appears that damages may be substantial. You have received medical reports that strongly suggest permanent damage to your client's appearance and faculties, and since Susan Ames is very young, damages will extend over a long period. Now that the case is beginning to take shape in your own mind, you may wish to get some advice and approval for your ongoing conduct of the case. If you are a junior partner or associate in a firm, this means writing an internal memo or a "decision memo" to the partners supervising the case. Even if you are yourself supervising the case and have no superior and no partners interested in the case, preparing an internal memo is still a good idea because writing will clarify your thinking about the case and provide a foundation for later preparation of a trial brief should one become necessary.

Knowing Your Audience

(If you are yourself the only audience for this internal memo, you may wish to skip over this and the following section and proceed to the section "Organizing and Drafting an Internal Memo" on page 45.)

Who constitutes your audience for this memo? Obviously, it is an experienced lawyer, who you may assume has read the file memoranda in the case. Nevertheless, because your reader is responsible for a number of files and may not remember all the details, some summary of the facts may be necessary—a capsule of what you consider to be most important to the case. Once again, we want to remind you to be impartial. Do not attempt to "sell" your case; let the facts and law speak for themselves.

Use this internal memo to inform your superior of your view of the case and to obtain his or her support for the way you intend to conduct it in the immediate future. Keep in mind that the approval you get at this point is not an open-ended declaration of support for any decision you might make in the future, especially if any future decisions turn out badly. Clearly, the approval you obtain here relates only to the facts known to this point and the short-term strategy you are recommending, so you need to be careful not to go further in your recommendation than the evidence in the case warrants at this point. This is not a simple matter, and we will return to it below, but first we need to focus on the question of purpose.

Determining Your Purpose

Depending on your relationship to your readers, your purpose in writing an internal memo may range from presenting various reasoned alternative courses of action without drawing conclusions (you are asking for direction), to simply informing your readers of your intended course of action (you are asking for ratification of a decision already made). In-between lie a number of possible variations, such as asking for guidance or approval.

One thing that this kind of memo shares with the file memorandum is that it also makes a record for the future. For example, although we all hope that our decisions are usually right, no lawyer has a perfect track record; therefore, the internal "decision" memo makes a record not only of the fact that approval of a strategy was requested and obtained, but also of the facts and law on which the decision was based. It therefore has important historical significance in the case.

Accordingly, in setting out to write or dictate, you have two important things to consider. The first is to determine the specific purpose of the memo—to decide what level of approval is needed—and the second is how to present the information and your argument.

Ultimately, the decision that you must make about purpose depends on your relationship to the case and to the other lawyers in the firm involved in its management in some way. You may be nominally in charge, while the ultimate responsibility lies with the partner whose client you represent. For example, the partner who generally represents Mr. Ames and his company may have retained the responsibility for the outcome of this case; indeed, he or she can hardly escape it. Perhaps in your firm, the partner in charge of litigation has the ultimate responsibility for the handling of this case, while you are responsible for the day-to-day management of the case. In the above situation, your internal memo will likely be addressed to both partners, since they share the burden of the outcome with you. The burden is always heavy in negligence cases involving children, and if Ames is an important client of the firm, that is an extra burden. The point is that before you proceed any farther you must clarify who is responsible for what, to whom, and in what degree.

We have dwelled on purpose because we know you will soon discover through experience (if you have not already done so) that purpose bears heavily on the choices you must make with respect to how much information you will include in your memo, how much you will summarize, and how much you will leave out altogether. In the Ames case, let us suppose your relationship is such that the purpose of your memo lies between the extremes of information-as-a-courtesy (the writer requires no direction or approval) and a full report and analysis for the purpose of receiving instructions (the writer has no authority to proceed). You will need to exercise considerable judgment in deciding what choices to make. In the remainder of this chapter, we will suggest some choices that you might make in the Ames case.

We said earlier that your purpose in this memo is to inform, but it must also argue a position. Clearly, as a practicing lawyer (even when you are working under a more senior lawyer), your role is to *shape* the case in a coherent summary. Your first task, therefore, is to decide where you think you are in the case.

1. Does the case look like a winner?
2. What facts and law lead to that conclusion?
3. What facts present or missing are you worried about?
4. What further factual evidence do you need to nail down your case?
5. Where do you expect to get it?
6. Finally, and perhaps most important, what are the weaknesses in your case?

Once you have answered these questions, you have an outline of your argument, and you are ready to begin writing. But remember, you cannot begin to write until you know where you stand, even though *as you write the memo your position may gradually change because you are exploring your ideas in the writing process.*

Organizing and Drafting an Internal Memo

The form of the memorandum is the same as the previous ones. In this instance, you will address it not to *File* (unless you are the only reader) but to a partner or partners by name. Of course, you will indicate the case name and file number and the date of your memo. Although the headings may vary from firm to firm, we suggest you use these: *Facts, Law, Discussion,* and *Recommendation* (or perhaps, *Conclusion*).

As you draft, you will often find that your ideas and opinions develop and change as you write. *Don't fight this process.* It is the very reason why we urge you repeatedly to write several drafts of every document. This is particularly true of the *Discussion* section of your memo. After two or three efforts to draft a coherent statement of the facts and of applicable case and statutory law, you may find in the course of writing the *Discussion* section that you have changed your mind about the case and that what appeared to be open-and-shut in your favor is now found to be full of holes that urgently need plugging. Note that, although we suggested you start with a purpose to your memo, we also equally strongly urge you not to start with a conclusion and write backward from it. Do not consciously select the facts and law that support it. In the first place, if you do not give a balanced and unbiased summary of the case as you understand it, you lose the benefit of whatever valuable advice you might otherwise receive from your partners; and in the second place, you are also liable to end up in a great deal of hot water when it is discovered that you either overlooked or concealed significant weaknesses in your case.

Synthesizing the Facts: The *Fact* Section

In the *Fact* section, you should set out a summary of the *most relevant* facts, but do not include as full a narrative as in the file memoranda. Although details of the case are available to your readers in the file memoranda and you may assume that they have read the file memoranda, you should refresh their memory by repeating the basic facts. Do not force your readers to refer back to the file memoranda by making too brief a statement here; on the other hand, if you are going to repeat everything you included in the file memoranda, the file memoranda serve no purpose. The internal memo is supposed to be a *synthesis* of the information; therefore, it must operate at a higher cognitive level, and it must represent your grasp of the case.

The key characteristic of a good synthesis of the information is *coherence*: the statement of facts still constitutes a readable narrative, however short, and even more important, it supports your recommendation, where you apply the relevant law to the facts. This, as you know, is the real essence of what a lawyer does; he or she *interprets* the law in its application to a specific set of facts. Of course, the facts that you choose to state and the facts you choose to omit will quite obviously affect the judgment of the reader. When you include a fact, you are making a value judgment that it is consequential, and conversely when you omit it, you are concluding it is not important. In that way, your memo is both informational and persuasive.

When you are finished drafting and redrafting your statement of the facts, it will look something like the one on page 47.

Internal Memo: Sample *Statement of Facts*

Statement of Facts

Our client in this matter is John Ames, whose company we represent generally (see file 874862A). Mr. Ames's daughter Susan, aged 8 years and six months, was struck by her school bus in front of Brinkman School for the Impaired at about 7:55 A.M. on April 27. Susan is profoundly deaf and consequently attends the special school. Normally, a teacher is in charge when the bus, operated by Busarus, an independent private carrier, disembarks the children. It is not yet clear whether a teacher was supervising on this occasion. There is some evidence to indicate that Susan darted in front of the bus as it was about to leave the school's driveway and that she was struck by the bumper.

Susan was taken to Northeast Tampa General Hospital and admitted to the emergency room. She was treated there for serious injuries to her head, legs, and neck. She was transferred to Children's Hospital, where she was operated on. The next day she was examined by a pediatric ophthalmologist and by a plastic surgeon. Preliminary indications are that she will suffer some permanent scarring and possibly permanent injury and loss of faculties. The pediatrician has recommended she be examined by an ophthalmologist.

An investigator's report for the Welfare Department indicates that teachers have complained in the past about the drop-off and pick-up procedures of the bus company, but that these complaints have not been acted upon. The police report indicates the driver did not see Susan reach under the bus for the notebook she dropped and which slid under the front bumper. A teacher may have called to the driver from the front steps of the school, but her warning was too late.

Researching the Law: The *Law* Section

Now you are ready for the *Law* section of the memo. Here again, although you are summarizing briefly, make sure that you give a balanced view of the law. Since this is an internal memo, your research will not be exhaustive at this point, and you should make that clear. You should also be prepared to go back to the *Fact* section and add facts that have become relevant when you have looked at the law. A fact that you earlier thought insignificant may suddenly become important if, for example, you find that a statute or line of cases makes a distinction between seven- and eight-year-old children for purposes of determining contributory negligence. By all means, even though this is not a court document, use the standard citation rules of the Bluebook or whatever other citation manual may be in use in your jurisdiction.

This may be a good time to review what constitutes adequate legal research for the purposes of an internal memo. We have said that it may be less exhaustive than a trial memo or a brief, but this surely does not mean that it may be careless or that it may overlook significant issues. In other words, it must be as broad in coverage of the issues as an appellate brief, but it may be less intensive. You must bring to the surface all the relevant legal issues even though you will subsequently dismiss many of them that are found to have no significant bearing on the case.

Why should you bother to bring up in the memo legal issues that do not *seem* to apply? There are two very good reasons for this. The first is that you must show your readers you have considered every possibility for both plaintiff's and defendant's case. Do not leave your readers wondering whether you have considered, for example, the "safe place" rule in its application to the Ames case. It probably has no application, since—as you will find when you research it—it applies mainly to landlord-tenant cases. Nevertheless, a reader who has handled a case involving the safe place doctrine within the last twenty years or so will likely remember the rule without necessarily remembering every detail of its applicability. Don't leave the door open for the reader to ask you whether you have considered it; mention it and dispose of it.

The second reason is that facts can change. Sometimes new facts are discovered that raise new legal issues; sometimes facts are discovered to be wrong. For example, suppose that Florida, where the Ames case takes place, has a provision in its statute licensing special schools (let's call it Florida Statute §447.09, although Florida does not actually have such a provision) that says pupils at special schools for the handicapped shall not as a matter of law and regardless of their age or the circumstances of any occurrence be held to have been contributorily negligent, just as if they were too young or otherwise incompetent. In their wisdom, the legislators might also have included a balancing provision that limits the indirect liability of individual officers and directors of the school but not for their direct culpable acts. You will certainly include this statutory provision in your coverage of the legal issues. Consequently, you might choose to omit any mention of the line of Florida cases covering comparative negligence of children and of the handicapped. What would be the point? In fact, there is still a point, and here it is: suppose that you later discovered in your investigation that the Brinkman School was not in fact licensed under the statute and was not therefore subject to the provision of the statute mentioned above. Obviously, your omission of an important area of the applicable law is going to look like just that: an inexplicable omission. But including it will appear to be an *abundance of caution*, the lawyer's analogue of the Hippocratic oath.

How, therefore, should you proceed to make a comprehensive survey of the applicable law? The place to begin is with either *Corpus Juris Secundum (C.J.S.)* or *American Jurisprudence Second.* There are also state encyclopedias of law that can aid you in the first phase of your research. For example, in Florida, you would use *Florida Digest 2d.* In this phase, you are simply trying to uncover every possible legal issue, so the best way to proceed is to follow these steps:

1. Make a list of every legal topic that is suggested by the facts. Take your time, and let the ideas develop. Some of the ideas may seem to be of little value, but put them down anyway. Although they may turn out to be wrong, they may in turn suggest other topics that are relevant to your case. Let the associative capacity of your mind do its work.
2. Go through the indexes of the legal encyclopedias to find the section in which each topic appears. For example, under "Safe Place" in *C.J.S.*, you will find *Landlord and Tenant* as the section in which this topic is covered. This suggests that you have looked up a useless topic, but you may nevertheless wish to glance through the table of contents of the *Landlord and Tenant* section to make sure there is nothing you can use. Under negligence, you will find a number of potentially interesting topics, and you will have to do some reading before eliminating or downgrading some of them.
3. Read through the table of contents for each of the sections you have listed until you find the subsections that are applicable to your case. By this time, you will have identified the major legal issues in your case. List each issue on a separate sheet of paper. As you go through the case, these notes will form the foundation for your later trial memorandum or trial brief. (*Note*: Some lawyers prefer to use 5" x 8" cards.) They constitute a valuable record of what you have looked at, what you have retained, and what you have discarded. We will return to the subject of your notes in chapter 8, where briefs are discussed.
4. Reading the obviously relevant topics, such as gross negligence, will lead you from the general to the specific, from encyclopedic summary to cases and statutes and legislative histories, and so on. From the applicable subsections or paragraphs of the ency-

clopedias, note the cases and statutes footnoted, and give a brief summary (one or two sentences should usually be enough) of the subsection. As you move from this case to other cases in your practice, and then return to this case, your brief notes will almost instantly get you up to speed so that you do not waste valuable time trying to remember where you were in your research.

5. Finally, read at least the statutes and the headnotes of the cases cited, and, of course, make notes. At this point, you have enough of a grasp of the legal issues to write the *Law* section of your memo, although you must be aware that your task of research is far from complete. Whether it is even sufficient for the purposes of the internal memo is a question that you must ask yourself in the light of the purpose you have determined (see above) and the economic and other circumstances of the case. How much time you should spend on the case at this stage depends on all of these circumstances. If you are in doubt, we suggest you get advice from a senior member of your firm.

Interpreting the Law: The *Discussion* and *Recommendation* Sections

In writing the *Discussion* section, the task is interpretation: apply the law to the facts. As we all know, that is a deceptively simple statement that conceals the real complexity of the task. For the purposes of this memo, however, you do not need to make a persuasive argument why a particularly favorable line of cases applies to your facts, as you would in a trial memorandum. The purpose here, you should keep in mind, is not to persuade but to present a broad view of the case. You will be able to refine it later. Since this book is about writing and not about jurisprudence, we will not dwell on the subject, but instead we will offer two useful pieces of advice:

1. Remember to revise, revise, and revise again. The advice applies not only to the *Discussion* section, but the preceding sections as well. As you think through the discussion, you may find your perspective changing and what you want to emphasize in the *Fact* and *Law* sections of the memo will change as well.
2. Remember that revising does not mean simply changing word order or substituting one word for another. Be prepared to move or delete whole paragraphs. Unless you are willing to do that, your writing will never attain its most effective level.

Finally, your *Recommendation* (or *Conclusion*) will be an outgrowth of your discussion of the case. You will want to briefly summarize the position you are taking. You will, of course, want to recommend either trying the case or avoiding trial. You might very well want to recommend settlement if your discussion leads to the conclusion that you have a very weak case. For example, you might recommend presenting the insurance companies involved in the case with a strong picture of the damages and hoping for an offer of settlement in spite of the weak liability. Regardless of the main recommendation, you will certainly recommend some specific procedures at this point: drafting the complaint, preparing specific motions, drafting interrogatories, and so on.

Developing a Style

At this point in the process of writing the internal memo, you should have a second or third draft that is balanced, complete, and argues your position effectively. You may now, as you approach the task of editing your memo, consider matters of style. It is admittedly difficult to keep legal memoranda from being monotonous and predictable in tone. Everyone tends to use the same impersonal and objective style, sanctioned by time and repetition. One would like to be different, to insert something of oneself in the memorandum, brief, or letter. While it is possible to inject a personal style into legal texts, particularly correspondence, there is a serious danger the writer must avoid when trying to use one's personal voice: don't appear frivolous at the wrong time or in the wrong place. This warning is especially true for younger lawyers who have not yet established their credentials among the members of the bar community, both within and outside their firm. The best style, therefore, is one that does not intrude. Like a dark business suit with conservative tie, a standard style is not noticed because it does not call attention to itself. It avoids the unwanted impression that the writer is advertising himself or herself. Therefore, use caution! Dress your language conservatively but well, just as you dress yourself. Do not try for humor or poetic effect. The *bon mot* in the mouth of the law professor goes well because his audience is obliged to laugh or to be impressed. Your audience is under no such obligation.

With that caveat, we suggest that individuality is not entirely out of place if you remember that personal style needs to be expressed in originality of expression rather than in idiosyncrasy and colloquialism. Idiosyncratic or colloquial language attracts attention to you the writer and away from the important things you are saying; plain, readable language does the opposite. Nevertheless, not only do the trenchant phrase, the aphorism, the particularly apt metaphor enliven your discourse, but they also imprint themselves on the memory of the readers, who take away from your document the impression that you are apt to be right in whatever you are saying. Do use caution, but if you know your audience, you may use the trenchant phrase or vivid image to enliven your writing.

As a memo writer, you must take care not to fall into the error of writing for yourself as the sole audience. Of course, as the writer you are also the audience, but only in the sense that you stand in the place of the potential audience to whom your memo is addressed. Note that this is equally true when your memo is nominally addressed to the file. Be sure to maintain the distinction between facts that are established and those that are hoped or supposed to be true by using adjectives like *alleged* or by using verbs like *stated*. For example, we noted earlier that Dr. Jones in his medical report says, "the van was moving approximately twenty miles per hour." Obviously, that is not a provable fact, at least not yet. Always attribute information to the source so the reader can check to see exactly what was said or written as distinct from your summary of it.

As with most internal memos, the reader is a lawyer, so you are a specialist writing to a specialist with the same vocabulary and knowledge of the discourse that you have. The special problems you face in writing to a lay audience are absent here. Nevertheless, you should be aware that the reader always knows less about the case than you do, since he or she did not have the benefit of doing the research and study that led up to the file memoranda, and especially did not have the benefit of writing the file memoranda. The extra benefit you enjoy as a writer is a special familiarity with the facts. In writing the file memoranda, not only have you made a special place for the facts in your memory, but you have also *synthesized* the material, thus ensuring a rapid recall of the information in organized form. Because your reader does not have this benefit, make sure to provide some general background information at the beginning of your memo, and be careful not to omit needed detail.

Revising and Copyediting Your Memo

As with the file memorandum, you have now arrived at an important final task: you must edit your last draft before submitting it to word processing for final production. If at all possible, get another lawyer to read your final draft. Do not rely on the employees of the firm who spend their time processing one document after another to find your mistakes; they simply cannot. The responsibility for professional-looking documents always rests with the writer.

You might use the following checklist as you revise the substance of your internal memo.

Checklist: Internal Memo

Purpose

Have you not only informed your audience about the case, but also argued your position about the case?

Audience

Have you presented information so that other lawyers in your firm can understand it and read it easily?

Tone

Have you kept an objective, unemotional tone?

Organization

Have you included these or similar sections: standard memo heading, *Statement of Facts, Issues Presented, Discussion, Recommended Actions?*

Contents

1. Have you summarized the most relevant facts, not including a full narrative as in the file memorandum?
2. Have you summarized all the relevant legal issues even though you may dismiss some of them if they are found to have no legal bearing on the case? Is your discussion of legal issues comprehensive, although not detailed?
3. In your discussion, do you apply the law to facts, presenting a broad view of the case?

CHAPTER 6

The Art of Summarizing: A Letter to a Lawyer-Client

In the previous chapter, you prepared an internal decision memo that paved the way for the future conduct of the Ames case. Because of the careful work you did in preparing that memo, you have made the job of drafting pleadings and supplementary documents easier for yourself and everyone else working on the case.

Suppose you have now served all the defendants in the Ames case, and they have answered with a general denial and various other defenses. Perhaps they have interposed motions with respect to one or more of the defendants. In short, some of the usual pretrial maneuvering has begun, but you are still a long way from trial, both in terms of time and money.

At this point in your preparation, you should begin thinking about your client: specifically what he or she ought to be told about the case. (*Note:* Although we refer throughout to Mr. Ames as the client, he is only nominally the client; the real plaintiff, of course, is his minor daughter, for whom and in whose name he acts.) One of the most important problems you face in writing to clients is deciding just how much to tell them. You do not want to put yourself in the position of reporting every event, both because of the time involved and because telling your clients too much about the conduct of the case is as inappropriate as telling them too little. Telling them too much about the case will get them bogged down in details, and may even leave the impression that you are not in command of the case. On the other hand, you should be aware that one of the most frequent complaints about lawyers is that they do not keep their clients informed. Clients want to feel that they know what you are doing, but they do not want a great mass of detail. You must carefully summarize, giving your client the impression that you are concealing nothing, while avoiding the impression that you are simply a reporter.

You have written an internal memo that outlines the progress of the case so far, and you have received a response that approves your handling of it. In chapters 7 and 8 we will show you how to turn the information in your internal memo into a letter to your client. In this chapter we will temporarily take you from the Ames side of the case into the other camp: we will suppose that you represent the School Insurance and Surety Company (SISCO), the insurer of BSI, the school in the case. You are going to write a letter of advice to the general counsel of SISCO, who is a lawyer.

Special Requirements for Writing to a Lawyer-Client

Let us review what we have said about understanding the communication situation in the last chapter and see how it applies to this new writing task. We need to consider once again audience, purpose, and tone or style. When you write to the general counsel of your client, the audience is another lawyer. Although you will be writing lawyer to lawyer, as in the case of the internal memo, your approach will be very different because, in the first place, the general counsel of SISCO, the liability insurer of BSI, is not a member of your firm. This letter, although it will include much of the same information as the internal memo, has a different purpose. In the internal memo, the purpose is to give a balanced account of the case up to the moment of writing, to inform the partners to whom you are writing so that they could give their approval and advice about the conduct of the case.

When you write to the general counsel of SISCO, you are also going to give a balanced account of the case as it now stands. Since the general counsel is a lawyer, you will give a fuller account of the law and a more professional discussion than you would to a client who is not a lawyer. Does that mean you will conceal things from a nonlawyer client? No, most emphatically it does not. But you must recognize that the lawyer-client knows more about the law than the layperson, and his or her relationship to the case is different. Although you are in charge of the case, the fact is that the general counsel of a corporate client rarely sees his or her duties as merely selecting a lawyer to handle litigation and then stepping out of the case. The general counsels expect to have some strategic influence on the case. You may know more about the case, but the general counsel knows more about corporate policy and corporate needs. Moreover, there is a political aspect to the situation you must take into account. The general counsel expects to be told more than the layperson not only because he or she knows more about the law, but also because, as the chief legal officer of SISCO, he or she is a mediator between the trial counsel and the management of SISCO and is answerable to SISCO management for results. The last thing the general counsel wants, and therefore the last thing you want, is to be put in the embarrassing position of knowing too little about the case to give an effective summary of it to SISCO's management and board of directors. Thus, your purpose walks a thin line between, on the one hand, asking for approval and advice (a tactical error in dealing with a client, even one who is a lawyer), and, on the other hand, simply providing information about what you have learned and what it means. The former approach appears weak and underconfident; the latter appears high-handed.

Since your immediate audience is a lawyer, you might be excused for writing a highly technical letter full of Latin phrases, technical legal terms, and arcane references. You might be excused, but you should not do it anyway. Once again, you will have to walk a thin line between textual and stylistic alternatives. You should not use a lot of jargon in your letter because it is likely to be read by several people besides the general counsel and his or her staff. Copies of it may end up on the desks of the vice-president for claims and the vice-president controller, both of whom are concerned with estimating claim losses. Accordingly, your letter cannot be so technical that it cannot be understood by nonlawyers, nor so simply written that you appear to be talking down to the general counsel. It must accomplish the miracle of being a communication between lawyers that can be read and understood by anyone.

Determining Scope: Summarizing the Facts

Given the need for a rather complete statement of the facts and law governing the case, you may wonder why you cannot simply repeat the internal memo, making only the appropriate changes in form to change it from a memo to a letter. While that is a tempting idea, it is quite definitely wrong. *The internal memo contains both too much and too little information* to transfer directly into a letter to the general counsel. Remember that your internal memo was addressed to readers who had access to the file memoranda with their rather complete statement of facts. Since John Doe, the general counsel of SISCO, doesn't have access to your files, you will need to give a more complete statement of facts in your letter to him than was necessary in the internal memo. While you would not, for example, quote from the medical statements or from the report of the state investigator in the internal memo, you may want to do so in your letter to Mr. Doe.

What you are trying to achieve is a balance between the bare bones summary of your internal memo, where the object was to give an economical statement of the facts sufficient to support your approach to the case, and the detailed presentation of facts in your file memoranda. Doe is going to want some of the flavor of the case in order to be able to form an intuitive as well as reasoned conclusion about the substance of the case. Once again, the more you know about your audience the better. We can generalize about the objectives of general counsel of corporations that you may represent, but certainly there are important differences in approach that senior corporate legal officers may bring to their positions, depending largely upon their personalities, interests, and experience. For example, if general counsel was himself or herself a trial lawyer before accepting the corporate position, a career change that often occurs, counsel will want more facts than if he or she has had little or no trial experience. A counsel who is not an experienced trial lawyer will tend to rely more on your summary of the facts, but he or she may want a more detailed discussion of the statutory and case law.

Obviously, corporate lawyers have different personalities and approaches to their positions; some want to be very involved in the details of trial, supervising outside counsel closely, and sometimes sitting in at the trial. Others are more remote, desiring to hand over the trial to outside counsel and expecting to receive reports only when there is something important to tell. Much depends on the number of trials the corporation is involved in. If it is involved in an extensive list of cases, as most liability insurers are, the corporate counsel cannot be very close to every one of them, and he or she will tend to follow most closely those with the potential for the largest judgment against the company. In short, there is no substitute for getting to know the corporate counsel and where his or her interests lie. One thing you can do is ask the members of your firm what the corporate counsel has seemed to expect in the past. Additionally, if you expect to represent the corporation in the future, or if the potential judgment is large, as in the Ames case, you should make it a point to invite the corporate counsel to lunch and politely interrogate him or her. You will find that Doe and any other corporate counsel you may deal with in the future are as interested in letting you know what they want and need as you are in finding out.

Specifically, in the Ames case, because the facts are not really complicated, your statement of facts should be somewhat more complete than you would expect to find in the opinion of an appellate court case. There, every fact that has relevance to the holding of the court is usually reported, with no excess. The court's statement of facts is economical to the point of terseness. Keep in mind that appellate court opinions do not address every issue on the case, only those that are appealed. Hence, the statement of facts may run, depending on the nature of the case and the issues appealed, anywhere from two paragraphs to two or three pages—from as little as 100 words to as many as 1,000 or more. Your statement of facts will usually need to be a page or perhaps more, because unlike the appellate court, you do not know how the case will come out, so you cannot ignore any real issues. But, if you are going to err in the matter of providing information, err on the side of brevity. It is probably better in the long run to have counsel ask you for more details than to mutter to himself or herself that you provided a five-page letter when only two or three pages were expected.

Arguing the Legal Issues Briefly

In this letter, unlike your internal memo, you should avoid raising every possible legal issue. Stick to those that you are confident are relevant, and discard those of remote applicability. What, you may ask, will I do if it turns out that some newly discovered fact makes a legal issue suddenly relevant that was of no concern before? Of course, you will write another letter to the corporate counsel reporting that you have uncovered new facts that bring up a new legal issue. Do not allow counsel to think you have simply fallen over the new facts or ignored them in the first place. The impression you must give is that your constant effort to expose all the facts of the case has been unremitting and finally rewarded with an important discovery, even if it is an unfavorable one. You will then discuss the new issue and will state your considered opinion of how it affects the case. The impression that counsel will get is that you are diligent and analytical. The impression counsel would get, if you included that legal issue in your initial letter when there was no reasonable likelihood of it applying to the case, is that you lack judgment. Our advice is this: have confidence in your analysis of the case; if you don't think something is important, leave it out. Here is a useful tip: anytime the digest you are using refers to a case as a *landmark,* be sure to mention it. Corporate counsels have such a broad responsibility that they rarely have as deep a specialized knowledge of case law as law firm practitioners, who generally can narrow the focus of their practice much more. But, corporate counsels have the same continuing legal education requirements you do; they attend seminars and they read advance sheets. Therefore, if they are at all familiar with the law relating to gross negligence, what they are most likely to know is the landmark cases. Your failure to mention the case will make him or her suspicious of whether you have thoroughly done your homework, and, we might add, nothing is more pleasing to a corporate counsel and more exasperating than catching an expert in an error of omission. *Don't let that happen to you!*

As for separating the statement of the legal issues from the discussion of them, we recommend that you do not do it. One of the differences between a letter and a brief is that the letter is much less formal and rigid. The form of the brief is pretty well determined by custom and practice. The letter allows more latitude, and that means that the way you approach *organization* of the information is different. Your experience may be different, but many lawyers have found that treating the legal issue and the discussion of it as an organic unit makes the letter more effective. For example, you would state and discuss the issue of negligence of the bus driver before turning to the next issue, let us say, the issue of strict liability (if you have decided that is an issue) and its discussion, and so on until you have covered all the issues.

Closing the Letter

Finally, and this is critically important, you must *summarize*. Here, in the last paragraph or two of your letter, is where you demonstrate how good a lawyer you are; in the summary you tell the reader what is most important in the letter and formulate your sense of direction for the case. For example, you might say that you have little doubt, based on the way the facts have shaped up so far, that a court would find the driver, and therefore the bus company and its insurance company, negligent. Since your client is the insurer of the school not the bus company, you might then address the question of whether the school is liable for failure to supervise, and so on. Finally, you might recommend that the defendants meet to discuss the issue of joint liability and to prepare an offer of settlement. Because of the emotional factor in jury awards (you might safely assume the plaintiff will demand a jury trial), the potential exists for a large award of damages, and consequently all the defendants may want to consider settlement before incurring the expense of trial.

Your closing sentence should call for some action on the part of the corporate counsel, for example: "Please call me when you have given some thought to my recommendation. I think we should meet at your earliest convenience to discuss it."

Using Correct Form for the Letter

In analyzing the rhetorical effect of different purposes and different readers in this chapter, we have already given some consideration to style and how it affects the tone you want your letter to have. Let us now focus on some specifics of style that we need to keep in mind during the drafting of this rather difficult letter to SISCO's general counsel. One of the main differences between a memorandum and a letter is formality. The memorandum is generally perceived to be less formal than the letter. There is no particular inherent difference; it is a matter of convention, arising out of the way letters and memos have traditionally been used in business and professional correspondence. Memos are normally used for internal communications and letters for external communications.

The form of the business letter has been sanctified by a long history of usage. Although the block style has recently replaced the indented style as the preferred form, the traditional meaningless greeting *Dear Sir, Dear Mr.* ____, *Dear Mrs.* _____, *Dear Miss* _____ (*Ms.* is preferred by some) remains a requirement, as does the equally meaningless valediction *Sincerely,* or *Yours truly.* Nothing seems sillier than to conclude an unfriendly, perhaps even hostile letter to opposing counsel with the words *Yours truly,* but it is still the convention. There are, of course, times when it is acceptable to be unconventional, but in legal correspondence the moments are rare and reserved for the writer who has an unusual purpose and the experience to know when and how to violate convention.

Since the violation of convention is a deliberate breaking of rules, it stands to reason that we cannot supply a set of rules for doing it appropriately. Look at it this way: lawyers dress very conventionally because they do not want to call attention to themselves by their clothing and because the layperson expects that sort of appearance. Law is a conservative profession, one that philosophically accepts the conservative rule of *stare decisis.* Our habit of dress is the American approximation of the British barrister's gown and white wig, a symbolic expression of adherence to ancient principles. If you were to walk into the federal district court to try a case or argue a motion wearing a red golf shirt and white pants, you would clearly be sending a message. But whether you would have chosen the most effective means of getting the message across is questionable, depending upon all the circumstances. We do not recommend it, nor do we recommend violation of the conventions of form in professional correspondence except in rare cases.

In external correspondence, use either the newer block form or the indented form, as shown in the samples presented below, and do not depart from these unless you know exactly what you are doing.

We have previously discussed the use of conventional headings in internal memoranda to make it easier for anyone picking up the file to find a particular section he or she may be looking for. It may seem to you at times that it would be a good idea to include headings in letters to corporate counsels, but unless the letter is extraordinarily long, it is usually not done. We strongly recommend that you use paragraph organization without the aid of headings. Your letter should not be so long as to require them, although there will be exceptions. You may someday find yourself at the head of a team of lawyers trying a $200,000,000 antitrust case for one of the Fortune 500 companies. When that happens, you may find yourself writing letters so long that headings and even subheadings become necessary. No rule of writing is without exceptions—except the rule that you must always think about the needs of your readers.

Sample Letter 1: Block Form, Formal Style

May 15, 1992

Mr. John Doe
Vice-President, General Counsel
School Insurance and Surety Company
One Insurance Plaza
Lawrence, Kansas 66044

Dear Mr. Doe:

Re: Ames v. The Brinkman School
File #90-203L

I am writing to let you know what has taken place in the Ames case since our last conversation. We have undertaken a preliminary investigation of the facts, and although our investigation is incomplete, I can now give you an informed statement of the pertinent facts, as well as inform you of the further investigation we propose by way of informal interviews, depositions, and production of documents.

//

I believe that brings you fully up to date in this matter. If you have any questions or comments, please call me at your convenience.

Sincerely,
(Your Name)

Getting the Right Tone

When we speak of tone, we are talking about how the text itself conveys information about the writer. Take a look at the sample letters on these two pages and note the difference in tone in the salutation even before the letter begins. Note the corresponding difference between closing with *Sincerely* and *Cordially*. Obviously, the writer of letter 2 knows Mr. Doe a great deal better.

Note also the difference in tone of the beginning phrase in the body of the letter. Although both letters begin without a time-wasting preamble, letter 2 begins somewhat more abruptly. It does not introduce the subject matter as formally as letter 1. Is this not consistent with the difference between the way you customarily address friends and the way you address strangers? The element of politeness that you incorporate in addressing strangers is absent from letter 2. Evidently the

Sample Letter 2: Indented Form, Informal Style

May 15, 1992

Mr. John Doe
Vice-President, General Counsel
School Insurance and Surety Company
One Insurance Plaza
Lawrence, Kansas 66044

Dear John:

Re: Ames v. The Brinkman School
File #90-203L

The Ames case is moving along rather swiftly, so I want to give you a thorough update on the facts and law as we presently see the case. I will also fill you in on our proposed conduct of the case from here forward.

//

If you have any questions or comments, please call me.

Cordially,
(Your Name)

writer knows the reader well, well enough to dispense with the more formal conventional beginning. The difficulty of dealing with conventional beginnings is that readers get tired of reading them. Does that mean you should skip the introductory sentence in letter 1 ("I am writing to let you know what has taken place in the Ames case . . .") and plunge right in ("I want to give you a thorough update . . .") as the writer of letter 2 did? Probably not, because there are some disadvantages (as previously noted) to overturning convention. Once again, the decision depends on what you know about the audience. One reader might sigh with relief not to get another letter from one of the thirty-seven outside lawyers retained by his or her company that begins, "I am writing you to . . ." Another might think you are presumptuous and discourteous for failing to do so. The gains from overturning convention rarely outweigh the risk of erring, so we recommend you stick to the safe beginning—varying it as much as you can—unless you are *sure* of the advantage of the unconventional.

The rest of the letter will tend to follow easily from the right beginning. Avoid a shifting tone, one that begins formally and drifts into something less formal as it goes along. Conversely, do not let your formal but direct beginning drift into pomposity. How can you avoid this drift in tone? Simply by being conscious of it and revising when your syntax or word choices become inappropriate. (For more advice on this topic, see chapters 15 and 16.) In your first draft, concentrate on making choices about what to include and what to exclude as your first priority. In the second draft, you will need to pay more attention to coherence and direction of the letter, and at the same time, or even in a third draft, if that becomes necessary, pay attention to consistency of tone.

You will achieve consistency of tone if you simply read the letter to yourself and listen for words or phrases that sound as though they came from a different person. For example, if you didn't know Mr. Doe well, you may have chosen to address him and begin your letter as sample letter 2 on page 63 does. Then, having become absorbed in your writing, you have dictated or written that you "contemplated advising" him, etc. Is this too formal? Reasonable men and women could differ, but we would say it is. Business practice today avoids the ornate and formal expressions such as "we beg to advise" and "in compliance with your request." Instead, the executive or professional of today says, "we want you to know" and "as you asked us." Don't say "please furnish me with the following information." Instead, say, "please send me the following," or, "I will need the following." In short, the accepted tone of business correspondence is more informal, more like conversation, with a significant exception. That exception is in the use of colloquialisms such as slang and contractions, which are a normal part of speech. Generally speaking, even in an informal business letter, you must scrupulously avoid the use of colloquialisms. Business letters, even informal ones, are not social letters.

We will summarize the discussion of style and tone in this way: letters are always more formal than memos but less formal than briefs and opinions, and within the genre of letters there can be a broad range of formality depending on the style in which you write it. It is impossible to give a set of rules to ensure the result you want, but try always to observe this one rule in all your writing: do not think like a lawyer, think like a person. Trust your intuition—you will find it very reliable—and your knowledge of the reader. If necessary, when you are still gaining experience, read every sentence and ask yourself whether it is either too pompous or too conversational. If in doubt, try substituting another word or phrase and *listen* to the new sentence. Is it better? Is it more consistent with the paragraph and the letter as a whole? We apologize if that sounds painstaking, but it is axiomatic that the less well you know the reader the more he or she will be influenced not only by what you say but by how you say it. To be a successful lawyer, you must take pains over everything you write.

Writing Letters to Opposing Parties

Everything we said about writing a letter to Mr. Doe applies to a letter to an opposing counsel. It also applies to a letter to another lawyer outside your firm for any reason. *Always* use the letter form, never the memorandum form. Always remember the difference between writing to a lawyer and a letter to a layperson. Remember also that the meaning the reader gets, regardless of the meaning you intend, is gathered both from what you say and how you say it.

You may also have occasion to write to an opposing party, usually to indicate that you are representing someone in the case. For example, you, as the Ames counsel, might have learned from BSI that it is insured by SISCO. It would be appropriate to write directly to SISCO to inform it that you represent Mr. Ames and his daughter involving a claim of negligence against BSI and that you understand from BSI that SISCO insures the school against liability. Keep the letter very formal, even though you may be acquainted with the officer of SISCO you are writing to, and *keep it short.* Don't explain your case to the opposition. It is true that SISCO can get the same information as you through discovery, but you should never make it easy by telling the opposition what to look for. And don't assume because SISCO has always been represented by a particular firm that it must be represented by that firm in this case. SISCO's lawyers will write you in due course to inform you of its representation, just as you have written to SISCO.

Preparing the Final Copy of Your Letter

After you have drafted your letter, you should carefully review its contents. Use the checklist on page 66 to guide you in your revision.

Before you are quite finished with this letter, you need to think about one more thing: who needs to get copies and whether they are open or "blind" copies. An open copy is one that shows a list of recipients at the bottom of the letter, for example, *C: W. P. Smith.* A blind copy does not list recipients on the original letter, only on the file copy; or perhaps just the copies will list recipients if you do not want the addressee to know who has received copies but you want all those copied to know. Not to include a list of recipients on the original letter is not usually a matter of keeping a secret but rather a matter of convention; usually you do not reveal on the original who else in your own firm has received copies. Thus, you might send blind copies to two or three interested partners in your firm. On the other hand, if you want Mr. Doe to know that W. P. Smith, a senior partner in your firm, has received a copy, you would show that as an open

Checklist: Letter to a Lawyer-Client

Purpose

Have you informed the client of the status of the case to this point and made clear your opinion on the next step to take? Do you show your client that you are handling the case competently?

Audience

1. Have you investigated to determine the level of detail that the lawyer-client prefers?
2. Have you written the letter so that interested parties who are not lawyers could also understand it?

Tone

1. Have you used a businesslike but conversational tone?
2. Have you avoided colloquialisms?
3. Have you avoided pompous language?

Contents

1. Have you made a brief presentation of facts, generally not longer than a page?
2. Have you focused on the relevant legal issues, omitting those whose applicability is remote? Have you included landmark cases in your discussion?
3. Have you presented each legal issue and your discussion of it as an organic unit?
4. Have you formulated your ideas about the direction of the case in the conclusion of the letter?

Format

1. Have you used traditional letter conventions, e.g., salutation, closing?
2. Have you used indented or block format correctly?
3. Have you avoided using headings and instead kept your letter relatively short?

copy on the original. Since the word processing people in your firm do not know who should receive copies unless they get instructions, you must indicate what copies you want sent to whom and whether blind or not.

Here's a final word of advice: every time you write anything for external readers you represent not only yourself but the members of your firm; hence you are contributing to your firm's reputation.

Therefore, no one should ever receive a letter from you on your firm stationery unless it has had careful attention to tone and careful editing. In the long run, you will find it worth the trouble to take care in the quality of what you send out.

CHAPTER 7

Translating for the Layperson: Writing to Your Client

In the letter that you wrote for chapter 6, as counsel for SISCO, the liability insurer of BSI, your purpose was to inform and persuade your reader. Your reader was a lawyer, and you were trying to persuade him that your grasp of the Ames case was both correct and comprehensive—in short, that you were handling it competently. In this chapter, you prepare a letter to Mr. Ames as the lawyer representing him as plaintiff. You are showing that you remember the injunction we mentioned in chapter 6 to keep your client informed. As in chapter 6, your purpose is not merely to summarize the status of the case; you also want to employ some subtle persuasion that convinces your client you are handling his or her case competently. However, in writing to Mr. Ames, you are not writing to another lawyer, but to a layperson who does not know a demurrer from a cross complaint. How can you best explain the issues to your reader?

Writing You-Centered Letters

The correct approach to any correspondence, but particularly in dealing with clients who are not lawyers, is to write a you-centered letter. One of the things that most troubles clients about lawyers, and a reason why so many complaints are filed with bar association grievance committees, is that lawyers often forget who is employing them. Lawyers sometimes get so wrapped up in their practices that they forget that without clients there would be no lawyers. Specifically, clients often complain that lawyers do not return their telephone calls. It is true that some clients are unreasonable and expect you to drop whatever you're doing when they call—even to run back from the courthouse if you are handling a trial. Discounting unreasonable complaints, there is still a core of grievance against the bar generally based on the belief that lawyers do not give enough consideration to their clients. Therefore, the *dictum* you will want to follow in writing to clients is: always make your letters to clients you-centered.

The way that you make your letter you-centered is not by sprinkling it with the word *you*. Instead, you must deliver information that takes into account the client's perspective; you must put yourself in your client's place and achieve an understanding of his or her needs. Since the tone of a letter is often established in the first sentence after the salutation, think about how you can make that first sentence you-centered. Obviously, writing that "*I* wanted to let you know how your case is progressing" is not you-centered; it is *I*-centered, it is about what *I* want to accomplish. A much better beginning is this: "Since we spoke last week, something has occurred in your case which you will find both interesting and, I hope, pleasing." This letter is going to be about the client and what is important to him or her, not about what is important to the lawyer. You will note that it incidentally reminds your client that you called him or her only last week.

It is tactically smart to write to your nonlawyer-client when you have something important to say because then it is easier for you to write a you-centered letter. Sometimes you cannot wait for an important event to write about—some cases would keep you waiting forever for news that is both important and good—so occasionally you will have to make your letter you-centered some other way. You will think of several yourself, but here is one to get you started:

> Dear Mr. Ames:
>
> You have probably been wondering what has happened in your case since we last spoke, so here is an update.

Making your letter you-centered is even more important when you want your client to take some action. For example, suppose that you want to know what representations BSI made to Mr. Ames about busing students to the school when he enrolled Susan there. In a telephone conversation, you have asked him about this, and he has said he will send you his file, but he hasn't done so. In your updating letter to him, you might want to remind him. Would it be better to say, "Please send me your file on BSI as soon as possible," or to say this:

> As soon as you send me your file on BSI, I will be able to determine whether they have made any legally binding undertakings.

How your client benefits from sending you his file is much more apparent in the second approach than in the first.

Preparing to Write: Doing More Research

Let us say that you have received three important pieces of information about the case just before you plan to write Mr. Ames. The first is a report from a state investigator for the Florida Department of Education which says that BSI had its license revoked last year for violations unrelated to the busing of children to the school and that BSI has appealed the revocation. The second piece of information is a letter from SISCO's lawyers offering a settlement in the case. Naturally, these two events are closely connected, since SISCO's lawyers have received the same information you have, and their letter follows by three days the investigative report. Naturally, you are quite pleased at these developments, and eager to tell your client.

However, the third piece of information, which you must also pass along, is that the insurer of the bus company has failed and been placed under the supervision of the Florida Insurance Department. You read in the newspaper that the condition of the insurance company has deteriorated to the extent that it will be unable to pay claims in full, in fact, may be unable to pay more than 20 percent of claims. What is particularly troubling to you is that the offer of settlement from BSI's lawyers is based on part of the damages only, and leaves it open for you to recover from the bus company. Given these circumstances, will you want to settle?

Your task is not only to explain to Mr. Ames the significance of these events, but to recommend a course of action. Before writing to him, you will have some investigating and some thinking to do. Here are the steps you ought to take before drafting your letter to Ames:

1. Do a little more factual research in order to pin down the possible damages a little better. You may wish to give Ames some idea of what the case may bring in damages, while at the same time making it absolutely clear that you can give no assurances as to what the judge or jury will bring in as a finding.
2. Do some legal research aimed at determining whether any cases have considered the question of what happens when a special school like BSI loses its license. Among other things, it may be operating illegally. But what effect would revocation have on the provision we mentioned in chapter 5, which legislates away comparative negligence of pupils at such schools as well as legislating away the liability of officers and directors? Now you have four new questions presented:
   a. What is the effect of losing the license during a period of appeal from the administrative ruling?
   b. Can an eight-year-old be negligent? (There is also a subques-

tion: does the fact that Susan is deaf and has been specially schooled and protected all her life affect the answer to the main question?)

c. If the officers and directors are no longer immune from judgment under the statute, under what circumstances may they be held negligent for the acts or omissions of the school? Must the school be guilty of gross negligence? Must the officers and directors individually have notice of dangerous practices?
d. How serious are the problems of the bus company's insurers? What is the financial condition of the bus company itself?

What we have, it now appears, after the first pleasurable sense of imminent victory, is a case with more angles to it than a billiard tournament.

Clarifying Your Purpose

Here your purpose is both to inform and to persuade your client. The normal prudence of lawyers would also suggest that you are making a record with everything you write. In these litigious times, it is useful to keep in mind that clients who were happy when they were handed a settlement check may later read of a huge jury settlement in another case and decide they have been swindled, not just by the insurance company, but by their own lawyer as well.

Your purpose requires that you take a position on the settlement offer and argue it. However, arguing in this context does not mean that you should argue your position as you would in a brief. You cannot expect your client to be able to follow the full implications of what you say, since Mr. Ames is not a lawyer. Lawyers argue in enthymemes—incomplete syllogisms—that rely on the reader's knowledge of what supports the conclusions. Some of the premises may be understood and hence are missing, but laypersons do not know this. Take a simple example: if you said, "Defendant's motion cannot be allowed; this is a Rule 32 matter," the judge and presumably most lawyers in the jurisdiction would know what you are talking about; your client probably would not. Thus, you have the difficult task in writing to your client of being able to explain issues in a language your client can understand. Also, you do not want to say so much that you bore your client, and you do not want to say so little that you mystify what must be clear. Therefore, in order to explain why you are now concerned about the possibility of Susan's negligence when you were not before, you must say something about the statute and the revocation of BSI's license and about the school's appeal of the revocation. But you do not want to say so little that your client's decision—and ultimately he or she must either approve or disapprove what you recommend—is uninformed.

Prewriting Your Letter: Outlining the Legal Issues

There are many issues at this point in the Ames case. You do not know what the driver will say, what teachers watching might say, what the other children might say (if they are competent to testify), what a passerby might have seen. Could Susan have reached under the bus for something she dropped? Even if she was negligent, what percentage might a jury find for Susan's comparative negligence? You have a lot to think about, but eventually, and soon, you must write. Prewriting, the cognitive process that goes on before drafting, helps you make an organized presentation of the case and its wrinkles.

You cannot simplify and summarize for Mr. Ames until you have a fairly full statement of the problems to work from in your own notes. So, you should write notes for yourself about what the issues are and where your research takes you so far. Once you have this overview down on paper, you can make decisions about what to put in your letter, what to restate, and what to leave out. *Do not, however, proceed to write a full-scale brief.* First, your preparation of the case isn't yet completed and may never be completed if the case is settled. Second, writing up notes about issues is a less time-consuming process, and it will suffice for the purpose of the client letter, as well as be a useful resource if and when you do have to prepare a trial or appellate brief. Proceed, then, by outlining all of the issues that bear on the question of settlement. Now you have a foundation to work from.

The actual drafting of the letter is going to be relatively easy once you have established your priorities. You undoubtedly have enough material for a twenty-page letter, but you are not going to write twenty pages to your lay client—not, that is, if you expect to keep the client. You must look carefully at your list of the issues, and just as you will later when you write a trial brief, you must put them in order of importance. In other words, now is the time to make some sort of outline that visually expresses the hierarchy represented by legal issues and their evidentiary support. This is the way a typical outline looks:

I. Negligence of Carrier

  A. Fla. Stat. 2302.6 and cases.

  B. Evidence

    1. Statements of witnesses
    2. Police report
    3. Etc.

II. Negligence of School

  A. Direct

1. Fla. Stat. 4919.6(a) and (b) and cases
2. Evidence [etc.]

B. Indirect (through Busarus) [etc.]

C. Strict Liability

Before starting the actual first draft, you have some difficult choices to make. There are a great many issues that must be considered before making a decision on whether you want to consider a settlement offer. However, you should keep in your own mind and be sure to point out to your client that settlement negotiations often break down, sometimes are resumed again, and sometimes break down again (and again). Although the ethics of the bar require you to negotiate in good faith, you are not bound to a settlement figure until there is an agreement in principle, it has been reduced to writing, and it has been accepted by the court. Therefore, your letter, while extremely important in setting the stage for settlement, is not the final stroke.

Managing Length

As a rule of thumb, the letter to your client ought not to exceed three pages. That means, after taking away space for your letterhead, the address, salutation, caption, and signature lines, you have less than two and a half pages, or about 1,000 words. That is not very many words to accomplish what you want. You should not follow our suggestion slavishly, however. If you cannot cover everything you need to say in three pages, take more. Moreover, you must suit the length to your client's needs. You probably know something about your client, if not directly, then through your partners. Some clients want a great deal more detail than others, and you must give them what they want.

After considering all this, you will probably find that what you must do is skip quickly over the issues that are simple and for which the evidence is relatively one-sided. For example, you might cover Busarus's negligence in one sentence: "We have a pretty solid case against the bus company and its insurer based on the deposition of the driver and statements of the children on the bus." Next you will talk about the issues that are more problematic, and there are two ways to do this: (1) You can talk about the most serious first or the least serious first, or (2) you can put them in logical order if there is any. Any of these ways will work, but you will probably find that what works best is a combination of least serious first and logical order.

Ordering Arguments

In a trial or appellate brief, as we will discuss later on, it is usual to put one's strongest arguments first. The reason, of course, is that if you impress the judge with your first argument, he or she will be predisposed to accept your weaker arguments. Some lawyers will claim that the opposite is true: that you must leave the judge with your strongest argument in mind, and, therefore, it ought to go last. How you proceed in terms of order depends on whether you are recommending negotiating a settlement or simply rejecting the offer out of hand. If you think settlement on some terms within reasonable negotiating distance of your opponent's first offer is in your client's best interest, you might proceed from the simple and favorable issues to the complicated and unfavorable; in other words, you would start with what is good about the case and proceed to discuss what you are troubled about. This is normally the way you will proceed, because opponents' first offer is rarely their final offer, and trying cases is rarely better for your client than settling them.

However, you should also proceed logically. It does not make sense to go from the carrier's negligence to the issue of damages to the issue of the school's strict liability. There is an inherent order to these issues that your outline will reveal and that you will need to keep in mind. You may be least troubled about the issue of comparative negligence, but it makes no sense to mention it before you discuss the liability of the carrier and the school, and within these discussions, the subissues arising under them. Thus, the order that you will put the material into from your detailed outline will present fewer choices than you think when you first look at it.

How lengthy a treatment you give to each issue is a more difficult matter to decide. Once again, however, it is not as difficult as it might at first appear. First, you started with some idea of how long your letter is going to be overall. The body of the letter must contain a conclusion, so you need to allow space for that in addition to the conventional beginning and ending. Of course, you also need an opening paragraph that introduces the subject matter of the letter—as we said above, a good, you-centered beginning. The length of the letter is elastic, but certainly not infinitely elastic. Make an estimate of how many paragraphs it will take to cover the easy issues. If they take up a page, then what you have left is perhaps a page and a half or perhaps two pages. If there are two troublesome issues, you might allow yourself a tentative allocation of 400 words to each. That's not absolutely binding on you, but you will find that if you do not plan the length of the letter you will find yourself having to cut an eight-page letter down to three, and that is more difficult than submitting your letter to internal discipline from the beginning. You will be amazed at how economically you can write when you have to. Economy of style is a very good habit to acquire—judges love it—so begin practicing it here. (For more on the subject of readability and economy of expression, see chapter 16.)

Writing a Conclusion

The conclusion is the most important part of your letter, so allow plenty of time for drafting and revising it. As usual, you will have some choices to make on what to put in and what to leave out. Your strategy in the body of the letter has been to cover most of the issues, although some quite briefly, developing most completely those issues that are problematic. In your conclusion, you should follow the same strategy, only more so. That is, you can omit entirely any mention of those issues that you represented as being well settled (although, as we have pointed out, you should not represent any event as being beyond the realm of possibility in a trial). Your conclusion is not a summary of the body of the letter so much as a focus on what is critical: these are typically issues on which you have a real possibility of losing, and the issue of damages. With respect to damages, comparative negligence is an important issue. In this case, is there any possibility of comparative negligence? The answer to that question is buried in complications. Finally, there is the very important practical question of which of the defendants has the ability to pay a judgment and which is uncollectible.

Out of these elements you must construct a conclusion that *is* a conclusion, one that leads to a decision. This will require more than a paragraph because you will need at least one to pull together the problematic issues in a logical manner and then state your recommendation for further action. Actually, in this case, you may need three paragraphs. You might consider putting the liability and comparative negligence issues in one paragraph, the collectability question in another, and your recommendation in a final paragraph.

One issue we have not mentioned is the cost of trial. We have suggested that you keep the risk of trial ever present in the mind of your client as it ought to be in yours. As all lawyers know, you cannot be afraid to try cases, or you will develop a reputation for timidity, and the result will be offers of settlement that are unreasonably low. On the other hand, you must exercise reasonable caution for your clients, on whom the burden of the uncertainty and the cost of trial fall. Should you, therefore, give your client an estimate of the cost of trying the case? You will certainly be called on to do that in a face-to-face meeting with the client unless he or she is very unusual and excessively liberal, but we would not recommend that you provide an estimate in your letter. Until you get closer to trial, the cost is very uncertain, depending as it does to a large extent on the length of the trial, as yet unknown, and the amount of pretrial discovery and motions that will be necessary. Since you are going to be obliged to tell your client that you cannot give any but the roughest estimate of cost from this point forward, *it is best to do so in person*. Therefore, the final sentence of your letter should suggest that the client meet with you as soon as possible to discuss the offer and your response.

Why not simply suggest that Ames call you when he has read the letter and can give you his answer? First, no matter how well written your letter is, it cannot be as personal as a face-to-face meeting. (If you are not going to suggest a meeting, you will have to close your letter with the request that Ames call you and let you know whether he agrees with you or not. Avoid even the faintest possible suggestion of an ultimatum: either adopt my recommendation or I wash my hands of responsibility for the outcome. It is not politic to do so, and since you cannot possibly escape responsibility for the outcome, there is no point in allowing this suggestion to creep into your letter.) Second, you should not expect to make the decision about how to respond to the offer unilaterally, without the participation of the partners who have some connection to the client or to the case. Since this is a crucial decision, Ames is likely to feel that he is entitled to personal attention from you and other members of the firm. Since you do not want your client to feel neglected even for a moment, we strongly urge you to close your letter with a request for a meeting as soon as possible.

Achieving the Right Voice

As with all letters, the voice—or tone—of this letter to your client is very important. It must be friendly yet not too informal, businesslike and crisp yet not impersonal. How friendly the tone should be depends on how well you know Ames. You can signal this by the way you address him at the beginning and end. You may write either, *Dear Mr. Ames*, or *Dear John*. You may close with either *Sincerely*, or *Yours truly*, or the more casual *Cordially*. Then you must accordingly sign your name either *Rufus P. Hornblow* or simply *Rufe*. Either way you sign it, your name should be printed out in full beneath your handwritten signature. (In informal notes, you may very well skip the usual valediction, *Sincerely*, and simply write your name at the bottom of the note.)

If you know your addressee well, you may wish to put in a final one-sentence paragraph with a personal comment. You must use discretion; if you don't know your client well, a personal comment may seem out of place. However, even though you may know Ames well, avoid a tone of easy familiarity, such as you might use in inviting him to the firm's annual Christmas party. This is, after all, a business letter not a personal one. If Ames is a businessman or professional, he recognizes the difference and might react with some dismay to a letter from you about an important legal matter written in too casual a style. Colloquialisms or contractions also are too informal for use in a business letter.

Another writing problem that results in striking the wrong tone is the use of clichés and dead metaphors. A dead metaphor is one that has been used so much that its freshness is gone; it has become trite. For example, do not say, "Let's all get on the same page of the hymnbook," when what you mean is, let's have a consensus or a meeting of the minds or a firm mutual understanding. Do not use metaphors unless they are fresh and perfectly apt.

Preparing the Final Version of Your Letter

Editing, as always, is a critical last step for anything you write. Do, by all means, check your letter for readability, and, if necessary, refresh your recollection of how to achieve readability and clarity of expression by reviewing chapter 16. As usual, get someone else to read your letter for coherence and readability if you can. Always give it a last reading yourself before turning it over to word processing. Try to see if there is any place where you can shorten your letter without losing clarity.

Use the checklist to review your letter to a lay client. Be sure to check that all lawyers in your firm who should receive a copy of the letter get one. Leaving someone out of the distribution of a letter to a client can be expensive in terms of internal politics. When in doubt, send a copy. What about people outside your firm? It is unlikely you will want to send anyone outside your firm a copy, since you must concern yourself with protecting the lawyer-client privilege. However, if Ames has a personal lawyer outside your firm who referred the case to you and who has remained peripherally involved in the case, you might wish to copy him or her. Before you do so, we recommend you check your state's law on the lawyer-client privilege. You are unlikely to say anything that could be used as evidence; nevertheless, take some time to exercise the successful lawyer's abundance of caution.

If your letter is well written, you have informed your client of what he or she needs to know and you have probably persuaded the client to your point of view. In addition, you have given the client a favorable impression of your work. Your letters to your clients are among the few opportunities you have to impress on them what a competent attorney you are because they seldom see you at your other tasks. If you produce clear, effective letters, you have strengthened your tie to clients and solidified your reputation among your colleagues.

Checklist: Letter to a Nonlawyer-Client

Purpose

Have you informed the client of the status of the case to this point and made clear your opinion on the next step to take? Do you show your client that you are handling the case competently?

Audience

1. Have you made the letter you-centered, showing how you are responding to the needs of the client?
2. Have you explained the issues in the case in language your lay client can understand?

Tone

1. Have you made your tone more formal or less formal, depending on how well you know the client?
2. Have you kept a professional tone, even if you know the client well?

Prewriting

Have you listed all the issues and where your research takes you so far so that you are prepared to make a recommendation to your client?

Contents

1. Have you included enough information so that the client can make an informed decision about the action you recommend?
2. As a general rule, is your letter no longer than three pages?
3. Have you started by discussing simple, favorable issues and then proceeding to complicated, unfavorable ones (if you are recommending a settlement)? (You might proceed in the opposite direction if you are not proposing a settlement.)
4. Have you stated your recommendation in a few concluding paragraphs?

CHAPTER 8

Arguing the Issues: Writing a Trial Brief

In the preceding chapters, you have written letters presenting the case for the benefit of your clients—in chapter 6, a lawyer-client, and in chapter 7, a layperson. In those letters, your task was to analyze all of the relevant issues of fact and law together. You were both informing the reader and persuading him or her to your point of view. You were presenting a balanced analysis rather than a one-sided argument, so your client could judge the direction the case was taking. In this chapter, you will be undertaking a similar task, in that you must deal in issues of fact and law. However, you will find that the task of writing a trial brief is different in many ways from the writing tasks you have encountered so far.

Let us suppose that you have analyzed the case for yourself and your client, Mr. Ames, and that you and your partners are persuaded that you should explore the possibilities of a settlement before you have invested more time and more expense of pretrial discovery and further factual investigation. Counsel for SISCO, BSI's insurer, has proposed a settlement meeting in which its representatives and you will be present. The liability of the carrier, Busarus, will not be dealt with at this meeting. You have countered with a proposal that all parties meet to discuss settlement of all damages, subject to a subsequent meeting between the defendants' insurers to agree on the contribution of each. Your reason for this proposal, of course, is that you have some doubts about your ability to collect either from Busarus or its insurance company. Busarus's insurer is in liquidation under the management of the state insurance commissioner, and the bus company's financial statement on file with the department of transportation is not too impressive. In other words, your best defendants from a liability standpoint are questionable payers, and your best payers,

BSI and SISCO, have questionable liability that may be offset by comparative negligence. In the circumstances, you would be wise to concentrate on getting a favorable settlement. You might also note how the fortunes of the lawyer can change several times as new facts turn up during the handling of a matter, whether he or she is handling litigation, a merger, a divorce, or what have you.

Unfortunately for you, the settlement conference breaks down, since it is discovered that the financially strong defendants have a very different idea from yours on an appropriate settlement figure, and the financially weak ones have a very different idea from that of the strong defendants over the appropriate burden for each in the settlement. As often happens, then, the conference breaks down over the subject of money, and the lawyers grimly pack up their briefcases and leave with their clients.

The Nature of a Trial Brief

Now let us further suppose that, after the settlement efforts have terminated, pretrial maneuvering has proceeded apace. A pretrial conference with the judge has been held in which the efforts at settlement have been discussed, the issues raised by the pleadings considered, and the length of the trial and other matters have been duly disposed of.

Judge Emily Stokes Madison, an experienced trial judge, has asked counsel for a trial brief on the issue of Florida Statutes §447.09. (You may recall this is the fictional Florida statute mentioned in chapter 5 that says pupils at special schools for the handicapped shall not as a matter of law and regardless of their age or the circumstances of any occurrence be held to have been contributorily negligent, just as if they were too young or otherwise incompetent.) She has also asked for information on the controversial provision for limiting liability in cases like this one and how it is affected by the revocation of BSI's license. While the legal questions are not unique, Judge Madison notes there have been few appellate cases in Florida under that particular provision, and none that presents all of the same questions as the Ames case. You and counsel for the defendants have been given a week to submit briefs.

Trial briefs differ from the memoranda and letters you have written in previous chapters in significant ways. First, the audience for a trial brief is quite obviously the judge, not another practicing lawyer or a client. The judge has no personal interest in the case; he or she is literally unbiased, and is influenced only by the briefs and what he or she knows of the law.

Second, you will not be dealing with all the issues as you did in the earlier documents. Judge Madison has clearly defined the limited purpose of the trial brief.

Third, you will be in an *adversarial mode*. Generally speaking, the Anglo-American judicial system relies on the dialectic between opposing counsel to arrive both at the facts and at the correct application of law. Although the Canon of Ethics requires counsel to be truthful in his or her presentation, professional ethics do not require counsel to adopt the opponent's point of view. Thus, if a case is found which is damaging to plaintiff, plaintiff's counsel is bound to acknowledge its existence, but not to concede its applicability to the facts of the case. Plaintiff's counsel must attempt to the best of his or her ability to distinguish the holding of that case from his or her own by analyzing the judicial purpose served and showing how the facts of the current case demand a different result for justice's sake. Of course, the counsel will not always succeed, but at least must try. The counsel cannot say, "Plaintiff has no viable cause of action because of the rule in *Blue v. Black,* 440 F.2d 996 (6th Cir. 1970)." The lawyer would not be giving the client the level of representation to which every client is entitled, and, in fact, the lawyer might very well be running the risk of being sued by defendants for bringing a frivolous action and by his or her client for malpractice. If *Blue v. Black* really is a killer case, counsel would have been obliged to find it out before filing suit. In short, counsel must present all sides of the case but argue effectively why his or her side is the better and the opposing counsel's side the worse. Out of that debate should come, in theory, the proper judicial decision, and it usually does.

Unlike a memorandum, the trial brief starts from a conclusion and pulls together arguments in support of that conclusion. The memorandum writer, as we pointed out earlier, starts with an open mind and analyzes the various issues, exposing all the arguments without bias. In contrast, the writer of a brief starts from the conclusion that his or her client's position is the right one, that it is on balance not merely the better argument but the overwhelmingly strongest case.

Your purpose in the trial brief is, therefore, no different from what it will be later in an appellate brief on the same issues. *Focus* is different, however, in that in the trial brief you rely on the facts you intend to prove, while in the appellate brief you have the transcript of the trial to work from. The attention of the appellate court is likely to attach itself more to public policy issues, to the ultimate effects of the rule it will enunciate than to the evidence, unless of course there is a question presented whether particular evidence should have been admitted or excluded.

Analyzing Audience for the Trial Brief: The Judge

We have consistently talked about audience with respect to every document we have prepared ourselves to write, and audience is particularly important for the trial brief. We need to ask ourselves, what is different about a judge as audience from any other lawyer? (We are assuming Judge Madison is a lawyer, although in some jurisdictions people have been elected to lower courts who are not lawyers. In those rare cases, you will have to treat the judge as somewhere between lawyer and layperson. You will have to assume that the lay judge knows more about the law than the average viewer of lawyers on television, but knows less than experienced lawyers, unless the judge has been on the bench a long time.)

Trial judges have heavy, varied caseloads, and they cannot be constantly abreast of the new cases in every area of the law. Judges must rely on counsel to present the novel or complex issues fully and accurately in trial briefs so that they can rule correctly on matters of law and instruct the jury (if there is one) properly. What this means to trial counsel is that his or her audience knows a great deal about the law but much less than trial counsel about the issues of the case. It also means, however, that the judge does not have a lot of time to spend reading briefs, so counsel must take these points into consideration:

1. Get to the point quickly.
2. Raise arguments very effectively.
3. Since this is an adversary process, *anticipate and refute* opposing counsel's argument.

You are now faced with writing a trial brief in a short time, as well as needing to continue to prepare for trial, so you must now make some important decisions about the scope of the brief. To meet this rhetorical and professional burden, you must walk a fine line between providing irrelevancies and failing to give the judge the strongest possible arguments—in other words, between saying too much and too little.

Prewriting the Trial Brief: Reviewing Facts

Always begin every writing task with prewriting, that part of the writing process devoted to organizing your thoughts on paper. The scope of your brief has already been broadly defined by Judge Madison, so you must start with that. You must address these issues: (1) What is the effect of the undisputed fact that BSI's license has been revoked for noncompliance with Florida laws other than the licensing statute itself? (2) *If* the effect of the revocation is to discharge BSI fully from the operation of the licensing statute, so that defendant isn't barred from introducing plaintiff's comparative negligence, then what is the state of the law with respect to the capacity of Susan to be negligent at all?

Now you must ask yourself, are these the only questions I need to research, or is there more hiding behind the two main questions? The answer, as is usually the case, is that there may be more relevant questions. Examine the facts first in simplified form. Listing the facts in summary form gives you a chance to review the strategy of the case, and you can then determine what part of the overall strategy you need to cover in the brief.

1. Susan Ames was struck by the Busarus bus in the driveway in front of BSI.
2. The unloading of pupils may or may not have occurred under the supervision of a BSI teacher assigned to supervise unloading. (In her deposition, Miss Gump, a teacher who was outside when Susan was struck by the bus, admits that she was watching the pupils leave the bus and enter the school, but was vague and evasive about whether she or another teacher regularly did so, and whether it was the school's usual practice to provide supervision for the pupils leaving the bus.)
3. Susan darted in front of the bus as it started to leave. Susan was eight years and six months old at the time, and because she was born deaf, has attended special schools since she was three years old.
4. BSI claims Busarus is an independent contractor, although Busarus provides a specific driver for all BSI trips, and the driver has been carefully vetted and approved by BSI.
5. BSI's license was revoked by the state for failure to adopt state regulations regarding minority hiring practices in hiring teachers, even after repeated warnings from the state's civil rights commission.
6. BSI has appealed from the revocation to the state's supreme court, and the appeal is now pending.

Are all of these facts relevant? They are all surely relevant to the trial of the case, but they do not all seem to be relevant to the particular issues that you must address in the trial brief. Selecting facts and applicable rules is always a contingent and ongoing process, because the rules that you may decide to apply depend on the facts you select, and the facts you select depend on what rules are relevant. The key to breaking out of this logical circle is beginning with what you are fairly certain of and making changes as your grasp of the problem opens and closes avenues of argument. In other words, as we have said before, writing is always a process of learning, which is why we place so much emphasis on writing several drafts.

Formatting of Briefs

Different forms of briefs require different formats, which may differ slightly from jurisdiction to jurisdiction. You must become familiar with the forms in use in your jurisdiction. One way to do so is to obtain from the clerks of the courts in which you practice or intend to practice copies of various documents that have been filed in the clerk's office. The trial brief is much less formal than the appellate brief, omitting the tables of authorities cited and statutes and regulations involved, but including the questions presented, the statement of facts, and the arguments. Both the appellate brief and the trial brief will have a formal conclusion, although in some jurisdictions the trial brief (also sometimes referred to as a Memorandum of Law when it is in support of a motion) will not. The trial brief lacks a formal title page, and usually looks like a form of pleading.

First Page of a Trial Brief

COUNTY COURT
STATE OF FLORIDA
LAKE COUNTY

JOHN HENRY AMES, Plaintiff	))))	 CIVIL ACTION NO. 91-478
v.		
 SCHOOL INSURANCE AND SURETY COMPANY, INC., et al., Defendants)	)))	Judge Emily Madison

---

TRIAL BRIEF
Questions Presented

//

Prewriting the Brief: Researching the Law

What is important in the trial brief is not the form but the substance of the brief. The overwhelmingly popular method with successful practitioners is to start by outlining the issues and rules. You begin the outline, of course, with *Questions Presented.* These are the questions submitted by the judge, and they will constitute the main headings of your outline for the brief. For each question or issue, you then provide the accepted rule. For main issues, this will seldom be in doubt, and you can cite the landmark case that supports each issue.

What you must do next is determine what subissues are presented by the main issues. For example, issue I is the question of whether revocation of a license issued under Florida Statutes 447.09 cancels all the provisions of that chapter of the laws, or whether it leaves some in effect. There are several subissues. For example, the rule for the main issue may be well settled that revocation of a license under several other sections of the Florida laws revokes all the provisions of that section. When, for example, you lose your license as an attorney under the Florida laws, you lose every right as an attorney. You would cite that as the main rule in Florida and then cite the cases that support it. However, it might happen that there are no cases reported under section 447.09. What do you do then? If your case requires the application of the main rule, you would argue by analogy from the other cases. You would show how public policy is similarly served by applying the same rule to the facts of this case. If you are representing Ames, is that what you want? Probably not, because what you might gain in being able to hold officers and directors liable—if in fact you have a case against them—is probably outweighed by the comparative negligence issue. That, of course, is something you would have to decide on the facts of the case, and what you know about the ability of proposed defendants to pay a judgment.

Another subissue is presented by the legislative history. Perhaps the history suggests that the legislature considered the question and failed to resolve it. In that case, you might try to read the history favorably to yourself, but you will have to recognize that opposing counsel will read it differently. Since the different defendants are represented by separate counsels, they may each read the history differently from you and from each other, since their interests are not identical. It may be necessary to turn to one of the digests, or to law review articles, or to a book on the subject by a noted authority. Having done this research, you may now find that some new fact that you were going to leave out of the statement of facts has become relevant and must be included. Make a note of it, because when you have finished your outline, your next step will be to write the statement of facts.

In this way, you will move down your outline, stating main issues, the rules, noting the citations, then developing the subissues, their rules, and their citations, until you have reached the end of the possibilities. You might infer that for every issue there is a rule, and that the rule is always unassailable and favorable. But, unfortunately, that inference is incorrect. In the first place, there are many legal questions for which no clear answers have developed. You may find that one of the *Questions Presented* has been chosen by the trial judge because he or she doesn't know the answer, and the judge doesn't know the answer because no one else does either. In doing your research, you may find that there are no cases reported in your jurisdiction that are remotely relevant; the digest doesn't even mention the problem; the noted authority presents a rule, but it is supported mainly by the weight of his or her years, and not by precedent; and four law review articles have been written in the last four years, each attacking the others and the noted authority. That's the bad news. The good news is that the way lies open for you to take the law review article most favorable to your case and cite it, calling attention to its applicability to the facts of your case.

Should you ignore unfavorable articles? Of course not. You want to impress on the judge the thoroughness of your research, but more important, you never want to let opposing counsel cite a case or authority that is relevant and can be turned to your disadvantage without your having dealt with it. Having "dealt with it" means having destroyed, if at all possible, its argument against your case. In other words, never ignore the unfavorable authority; always attempt to distinguish it or discredit it. In this case, you can discredit opposing views by adopting the argument of the law review articles that have attacked the unfavorable authorities. You should be able to discredit all the other unfavorable opinions in the same way.

Nevertheless, you may have a sinking feeling about this issue. After all, you may tell yourself, the other side can do to me what I have done to them. This is true. The antidote for this particular sinking feeling is to do two things. Even if it is now 3:00 A.M. of the morning on which the brief must be submitted, go back over everything and make certain you have not missed some weakness in the argument of the authorities lined up against you. Perhaps there is some little difference in the facts of your case that presents a different lever to public policy; perhaps some premise in a long string of conclusions presented in some opinion is incorrect. When you have done that last study and submitted it to internal argument, all you can do is hope for the best and begin to write the brief so that you will have time to edit it before it must be printed.

Lawyers must always remind themselves, whatever the case and whatever the hour, that no rule is unassailable, whether it is for you or against you, and quite obviously some rules are obliquely for or against you. If the cases that favor you are assailable, so are those that are against you. You must address all of them, showing how the favorable ones apply and how the unfavorable ones do not. Typically, there will not be very many cases, and they will be nicely digested for you. When they are not, you will have to do the work yourself. *Reminder:* Headnotes are almost always reliable, but note that we said "almost." Once in a great while, a headnote is wrong, perhaps even contrary to the actual holding of the case. Always read the opinions yourself, using headnotes only to determine what if any issues raised by a case are relevant to yours.

Drafting the Brief

The time and effort involved in writing a brief is concentrated in the prewriting stage. In fact, it is usually difficult to tell where prewriting ends and writing begins, because when you have completed a good, detailed outline of your argument, the writing goes very quickly. The first draft will go very much more quickly if you have followed our advice in chapter 5 to put each of the issues you were researching on separate sheets or cards. Since you now have done a thorough job of researching the two main issues of the trial brief, you can use your notes as the basis for your first draft.

The first draft consists of putting your notes into grammatical, readable English. Phrases that you wrote in your notes, for example, "Dillon case 6yrs. old could not be negl.," must now be converted into full sentences: "The holding of *Metropolitan Dade County v. Dillon* was that a girl, six years old, could not be contributorily negligent, even though it appeared that the child had deliberately darted under the wheels of a truck to retrieve her lunch box."

A logical structure is the goal of a well-written brief. The format is a given: heading, facts, argument, conclusion, in that order. The facts should be laid out with only as much detail as you think is absolutely necessary; in other words, do not put in one unnecessary word. Trial judges are, as noted before, busy and therefore unwilling to spend time leafing through an unnecessarily wordy brief. For this reason, good strategy dictates that you use plenty of paragraphs to break up the statement of facts. A paragraph in the statement of facts should rarely exceed a third of a page, and two sentences is not too short.

Logical structure in the *Argument* section normally proceeds from the general to the particular: (1) from statutes, when applicable (2) to case law (3) to legislative history (4) to other authorities. The license revocation issue in the Ames case involves a statute; therefore, you would proceed by arguing from the language of the statute itself, to the cases you would find by referring perhaps to *Florida Statutes Annotated*, and whatever additional cases you found by tracking those cases through a citator.

What you have now is a mass of notes, containing snatches from appellate case opinions, digests, articles, and books. If you use one of the drafting strategies we recommend in chapter 2, it should be relatively easy as a next step to try to state a rule out of this, all of its exceptions, and all of its contrary holdings. This may require several sentences, each buttressed by citations to cases and authorities. Always move from the rule itself to the exceptions and minority points of view. You must show (1) either how the main rule applies to your case, and then you must distinguish the exceptions and minority opinions on the basis of facts, or on the basis that an older rule has been overcome by a newer rule (assuming the dates of cases support that view); (2) or how the exception or minority rule applies on the basis of the facts of your case.

Be careful that connected ideas are closely situated in the text. Having stated Issue I, do not proceed from subissue A to subissue B and then back to subissue A. If your outline follows the plan we have suggested above, you can simply follow it, going from I.A.1. to I.A.2. in your outline through to the end of I.A, then I.B., and so on to the end of I, and from the beginning to the end of II.

Appropriate Style for a Brief

Good brief writing must be both readable and economical. According to convention, briefs rarely use any but the plainest possible language, completely unornamented. The result is that briefs are often not very interesting documents to read, and there are some lawyers who would like to change the conventions to allow freer use of language in legal documents. As of this writing, however, we know of no one who would recommend that you depart from convention. On the contrary, we would recommend that you use short, clear sentences, each containing a proposition, followed by a citation wherever necessary, particularly if the proposition is a quotation from a statute or case. It sounds somewhat choppy to the ear, but it *promotes economy.* You say no more than you have to, even to give the language the flowing sound it has when written by a good writer.

Here is a perfect example of good writing style for a brief:

> I. SEPARATING THE ISSUES FOR TRIAL WOULD PROMOTE CONVENIENCE, AVOID PREJUDICE, AND SERVE THE INTEREST OF EXPEDITION.
>
> Rule 9 of the Rules of Civil Procedure provides that the court may, "in furtherance of convenience, or to avoid prejudice," order a separate trial of any issue. Bifurcation of issues is indicated in cases where liability is doubtful, or where a simpler issue, that is dispositive of the case, can be tried first. *Matter of Johnson*, 675 So.2d 225 (1987). See 42 Florida L. Rev. 636 (1965).
>
> The grounds for bifurcation, convenience, avoidance of prejudice, and conduciveness to expedition and economy, are in the alternative. Thus, proof of any one of these grounds is sufficient to sustain an order for a separate trial. *Blankenship v. Precious Metals Corp.*, 498 So.2d 476 (1979).

The brief will go on like that until the end, merely an expansion into full sentences of your detailed outline. Although the language is not very interesting, it is readable and sparing in its use of words. Most important, it provides what the reader wants. Note, incidentally, that the reader's time is saved by the convention of restating the question presented at the beginning of the brief as a positive or negative statement at the beginning of the argument. It should be typed in all capitals to make it stand out.

Revising the Brief

After you have completed each draft, read it over for logic. Closely review the *Argument* section: make sure that there are no holdings or opinions or commentaries that do not lead somewhere. Everything must be connected: everything you insert into your argument must support, modify, or contradict something else.

Your argument may have some very long sentences, with many subordinate clauses, and strings of commas. When you have a long sentence with subordinate clauses marked by commas, give some thought to separating the ideas into two or three sentences to improve readability. Avoid using long sentences unless a series of shorter sentences seems to needlessly break up related thoughts.

In revising your brief, you can use the checklist on the following page to see if you followed the key criteria in writing your trial brief.

Checklist: A Trial Brief

Purpose

Have you argued your side of the legal questions posed by the judge? Have you refuted opposing arguments?

Audience

Have you written for a professional audience who wants the issues presented concisely?

Tone

Have you used the standard impersonal tone?

Prewriting

1. Have you determined which facts are relevant to the issues?
2. Have you researched the issues and identified all the subissues?

Contents

1. Are your arguments structured in this way: issue, rule, application, and conclusion?
2. Have you anticipated and refuted opposing counsel's arguments?
3. Have you tried to answer unfavorable authorities by distinguishing them from your case or by discrediting them?
4. Does the brief contain short, clear sentences, each with a proposition, followed by a citation where necessary?
5. Is the brief concise and written in plain language?

Format

Have you followed the format used in the jurisdiction? Typically this includes *Questions Presented, Statement of Facts, Arguments,* and *Conclusion.*

CHAPTER 9

A Delicate Assignment: Writing a Legal Opinion

Although writing a brief requires a great deal of skill and effort, writing a legal opinion is an even more demanding task. When you agree to write a legal opinion, you put your professional reputation as a lawyer on the line more directly than you do when writing a brief.

The Purpose of a Legal Opinion

Writing a legal opinion requires all the research and draftsmanship of a brief and all the rhetorical skill of writing a letter to a client. In a brief you need to argue your side of a case as effectively as you can. But when you write an opinion for a client, you must state your interpretation of what the law is and the probable outcome of the case, given the facts as known or assumed to be. You are in a similar position to a judge writing an appellate opinion, with two important differences. The first is that the judge's opinion is not going to be put to the same test as yours. If you are wrong, your client may suffer adverse consequences, some of which may be visited on you. When the appellate judge is wrong, the only consequence is that the opinion may be overturned. The second difference is that the appellate judge has a record of the facts in the trial transcript. Although you may think you know the facts, the information your client gave you may turn out to be incorrect, your own investigation may not have discovered the complete truth, or the facts, as is often the case, cannot be established with absolute certainty.

For these reasons, and the additional reason that trials are notoriously chancy affairs, most lawyers are careful about what legal opinions they agree to write. Even when you have agreed to write an opinion, perhaps because your client has insisted on it, you must protect your client, yourself, and your firm by wording it very carefully.

You might want to keep in mind that the Canon of Ethics, far from encouraging lawyers to give absolute or even unguarded assurances to their clients, admonishes lawyers to be wary of giving such assurances.

Very likely, as the lawyer for SISCO in the Ames case, these thoughts would flash through your mind if you were asked by the general counsel of SISCO, Mr. John Doe (to whom you wrote an updating letter in chapter 6), to write what is commonly called an evaluation letter. In the insurance industry, requests for evaluation letters are quite common, and they are used at financial reporting dates in determining the liability of the insurance company for outstanding claims. The evaluation letter is a form of opinion letter in which a lawyer not only gives his or her opinion as to legal liability but also gives an estimate of the possible damage award if the client is found liable. Often, the lawyer writing it will also give an opinion on what a settlement amount might be.

Let us assume that the Ames trial is still some weeks away, and Mr. Doe of SISCO has asked you for an evaluation letter to aid the company in determining its liabilities as of the quarter ending next Tuesday, four days away. Your letter will be dated as of Tuesday and must be delivered by at least the end of Wednesday. Although you are very familiar with the facts, and you have researched the issues, there are still some uncertainties of fact and law apart from the usual uncertainty provided by a jury trial. Today being Friday, and with a full schedule for today, including a hearing on a motion in another case, it looks as though you may be spending some of your weekend in the law library and either at your computer at the office or working on the laptop at home.

Opening an Opinion Letter

How should you begin this new writing assignment? You will need an opening sentence by way of introduction. In this case, the introductory sentence is simple and can be used in almost every opinion letter you write. You may say, "You have requested our opinion whether . . ." or "We have carefully examined the file in the captioned matter as you requested and are prepared to offer our evaluation." The second approach is rather indirect, but does give notice of the purpose and content of the letter. However, we prefer the most direct approach, as in the first opening. Even though, in this instance, the addressee will know the purpose of the letter as soon as he sees the caption *Ames v. BSI, et al.*, one can never be certain by whom else the letter will be read. It is probably prudent, therefore, to indicate that the letter of opinion is written at the client's request and to indicate your understanding of how it is to be used, as, for example, for obtaining an estimate of damages in connection with financial statements or for determining what course of action to take.

Some lawyers, when they know their client very well on a personal basis, consider it appropriate to write an opinion letter informally, even breezily, as if they were addressing the client on the telephone. They might begin, "So, you're in trouble again, and you want my advice about how to get out of the Jones contract. Well, here it is." That beginning would be very appropriate in the rare (we hope) case where you are helping out a friend with free advice, as all lawyers are occasionally asked to do. If that's the case, you should not be putting it in writing. Free opinions should be oral opinions given with extreme reluctance. On the other hand, if you're getting paid for this letter, then your reputation is on the line and your letter should reflect that it is a formal legal document by reading like one. Once again, remember that style reflects purpose.

Having settled on an introductory sentence, you should proceed directly to the body of the letter. Just as the purpose of a lawyer's opinion is similar to a judicial opinion, so is the structure. You will recite the facts, state your conclusion, and then provide the legal analysis in support of your conclusion.

Reciting the Facts

Your statement of facts must be as complete as necessary to support your argument. If there is any fact left out that would have made a difference, and your conclusion turns out to be wrong, then you are at fault. If you give a complete but condensed statement of facts—what you intend to prove, what you think your opponents can prove—and you lose the case because the jury finds differently, you are not at fault. When your client has supplied some of the information, you should specifically make reference to it, just in case some document he or she has given you has been superseded, or he or she has overlooked something important in the file, or a relevant document has been lost and you have not been informed of its loss or even of its existence. All of these things happen in the real world of legal practice, and you cannot count on your client for much more than this statement: "Oh, I meant to tell you that."

A careful job of reciting the facts on which the opinion is based is as important as a careful job of research and analysis of the law. Where the opinion rests on assumptions as to the truth of certain matters or when a fact has not been or cannot be established, note this. On the other hand, do not include irrelevant information. Just as in memo writing, what facts you include depends on what issues you consider relevant, and what issues you consider relevant depends on what the facts are. Thus, as we have pointed out above, the process is somewhat recursive and may require numerous revisions. One solution to this problem is to write the legal analysis first even though it will appear last in the letter. Once you have established what the issues are, and what kind of facts they may turn on, selecting the relevant facts to include in your letter will be easier. Since you cannot keep going in circles, you should begin with the issues, not the facts, and proceed in successive drafts to focus on what is finally critical and what is not.

Writing Your Opinion

You will, of course, write your conclusion about the matter at hand last. However, it will usually appear right after the facts—or even before them, at the beginning of the letter. Some lawyers vary where they place their opinion based on whether it is favorable or unfavorable to their clients. If it is good news, they suggest, put it right at the top. If it's bad news, give them your legal analysis first, so they will know how you arrived at your opinion before they read what it is. There is no rule that requires you to put the parts of an opinion letter in the order we suggest, and even the convention is rather loose, so you can order it anyway you want.

How strong a conclusion must you write? The obvious answer is the stronger the case, the more unequivocal the conclusion. However, the prudent lawyer never proclaims to his or her client that the case is unbeatable. Juries are no respecters of lawyers' opinions about the case, and the unexpected can always occur. However, when a client asks for your opinion, he or she expects some kind of answer. The penalty of too much certainty is obvious, so you must be more careful of your wording in writing an opinion in a doubtful case than in any other kind of writing you do. This doesn't mean you should indulge in the kind of double-talk that is the stock-in-trade of the stereotypical incompetent lawyer on television. You must say what you have to say clearly but without overstating or understating the chances of success.

Note that there is a sharp and important difference between "waffling"—vague and wavering statements—and stating uncertainty with clear language. Here is an example of waffling:

> Perhaps our best strategy would be to settle the case on some terms that we might negotiate with the defendant; on the other hand, I am prepared to go forward with this case and prosecute it with diligence if that is what you want.

No client with any sense will entrust his case to a lawyer who would write that sentence. An example of clear and forceful language is this:

> It is my opinion that we have a slightly better than even chance of winning this case. In expressing my opinion, I am relying on the

> evidence presently before us, including the information you have supplied yourself, as I have summarized it above. I am also taking note of the uncertain state of the law with respect to comparative negligence in this state, because of the relative newness of the comparative negligence statute and the paucity of cases, which I have analyzed above. *[Note that in this instance, the writer has provided the legal analysis before the conclusion because of the uncertainty of the conclusion.]* For this reason, I recommend that we attempt to settle the case without a trial. In my opinion, a settlement in our favor of $______ plus costs would be very favorable.

Note that the writer, in consideration of the uncertainty of the outcome, is recommending settlement, a very prudent thing to do when the case is doubtful. It does not necessarily follow that counsel for the opposition will agree; he or she may think the opposition has a wonderful case and may dare you to try it. Your job, of course, will be to convince your opponents of the strength of your case and the benefit to them of settling.

Writing the Legal Analysis

How much and what you write in the legal analysis—the argument that supports your opinion or conclusion—depends upon the audience. Knowing your client is the most important thing. Even if he or she is a layperson, your client may not want you to gloss over the legal analysis. If that is the case, then you must contrive to write it so readably that a lay client can understand what you are saying. Regardless of your client's wishes, you must always provide a legal analysis since you can never tell where your opinion letter will wind up being read and used once it leaves your hands. In the not-so-unlikely event that, in a losing case, your client objects to paying your bill because he or she says, "I thought we were going to win this case," you can show the client not only your carefully worded conclusion but also your thorough analysis of the facts and law.

This warning always to write a careful legal analysis applies with at least equal force when you are writing to clients who want an opinion about whether they can safely follow a contemplated course of action. They want your assurance that it is "all right." They will often add to this request the advice that you should "not bother with all that legal mumbo jumbo. Just give me your answer in English." You will certainly give them your answer, if you choose to write an opinion, and in readable English. But for your own protection, if not your clients', you will provide a thorough and complete justification for the conclusion you are going to express. That means reciting a complete statement of the facts as *the client presented them to you and a careful analysis of the law.*

How much analysis you must give depends on how complex the matter is. Naturally, you will not provide the same nicety of argument and wealth of authority that you would supply for a law review article on the issue, but you must supply enough to show that you have done your research carefully. You can do this by stating the main points in a coherent way that demonstrates what the issue is and how the courts have differed in dealing with it. If your client is a layperson, it is not necessary to cite authorities; the client will not be familiar with them, and he or she is unlikely to go to a law library to read them. The opposite is true when, as in this case, your addressee is a lawyer. For example, Mr. Doe of SISCO will want and expect you to cite legal authorities.

STRUCTURING THE LEGAL ANALYSIS

You must also decide on the order for your analysis. If, for example, there is a legal issue that could result in the case being dismissed, you would obviously raise that first. You would not, of course, stop there unless you are utterly certain that the case will be dismissed. Otherwise, you must explain how the case shapes up in the event it is not dismissed. If there is an issue that is highly doubtful, you may wish to begin with that, and treat the more routine issues, those that are well settled, last. Or you might treat them in the order in which they arise in the case. You will not be able to determine this until you have written a draft, read it back to yourself, and recognized that there is a logical order which seems to present itself.

For example, the structure of the legal analysis section of the letter to SISCO would be organized around three main issues: the alleged negligence of Busarus, the alleged negligence of BSI through agency, and the alleged negligence of BSI through its own conduct. Each of these has subissues. For example, there is the question of whether BSI's conduct might have abrogated the coverage of the policy. Your method of organizing this material may require outlining or some other organizing method discussed in Part I or Part III. (You will not usually find it necessary to outline the facts before writing that section—as you are by this time very familiar with the relevant facts of the case—or to outline the conclusion.)

For example, in the Ames case, as counsel for SISCO, you are not concerned about the liability of other defendants, so you would deal first with the liability of BSI, the insured, directly. As a subissue, you would then deal with the possibility that its negligence arises from a course of conduct that abrogates the terms of the insurance policy. It may be your considered opinion that the policy does not cover the negligence of BSI in this case, based on the facts. Even so, you must then proceed to cover the issues related to BSI's liability as the employer or principal of Busarus, because SISCO may be liable for coverage of the liability of BSI that arises in this way. So, this section of your analysis may read something like this:

> The distinction between an agent and an independent contractor is that the former is under the direction and control of the employer "with regard to the details of the engagement." *Gross v. Eustis Fruit Co.,* 160 So.2d 55 (1964, Fla App D2). Generally, the test of what constitutes independent service lies in the quality of the control exercised, "the decisive question being who has the right to direct what shall be done, and when and how it shall be done." *Collins v. Federated Mut. Implement and Hardware Ins. Co.,* 247 So.2d 461 (1971, Fla App D4). If the employer interferes or meddles with the job of the subcontractor to the extent of assuming the *detailed* direction of it, he may become the master of the contractor's employees. Fla Jur2d §109.
>
> The burden of proof is on the party asserting the relationship where there is no contractual evidence. This burden is not a light one. The courts have held that the mere suggestion by the employer as to details of work is not enough to change the relationship. See *Easton v. Weir,* 125 So.2d 115 (1960, Fla App D2), and the cases that follow it.

Since the liability of BSI, and hence that of your client, SISCO, may be derived from the liability of Busarus for negligence, you will need to treat that issue as well. In this case, the liability of the carrier cannot be disposed of quickly, because it is a private not a common carrier. Common carriers have what amounts to almost a strict liability for their passengers, including passengers alighting, but private carriers do not. You would begin this section somewhat like this:

> The general rule in Florida is that common carriers owe their passengers the highest degree of care. *[Cite leading case.]* However, the general rule does not "impose upon a private carrier a duty higher than ordinary care." Fla Jur2d *Carriers* §111. This section goes on to say that the rule "appears to be" that the carrier owes the highest degree of care when a passenger is entering or leaving the vehicle, citing *Atlantic Greyhound Lines v. Lovett,* 184 So. 133 (1938), and *Transit Casualty Company v. Puchalsky,* 382 So.2d 359 (1980, Fla App D5). A careful reading of these two cases and the more recent case of *[citation]* leads me to conclude that Busarus owed a higher than ordinary duty of care when Susan Ames was alighting from the bus.

You would then proceed to discuss the meaning of this level of care in the terms used by the appellate cases defining it, and how that level of care relates to the facts. Even for a lawyer-client, it is necessary to explain the meaning of "higher than ordinary care," because the term is somewhat ambiguous on its face, and none but an attorney practicing negligence law as a specialty is likely to be familiar with the defining cases. However, you must keep the explanation brief.

WRITING FOR THE LAY CLIENT

Dealing with the same question in an opinion letter to a lay client raises greater difficulties. This kind of lawyerly distinction among (1) ordinary care, (2) a higher duty than ordinary care, (3) strict liability, (4) gross negligence, and so forth, is the kind of language manipulation that a lawyer treats as routine and the public calls "legal nitpicking." It is not surprising that the public has difficulty with this kind of fine distinction; many lawyers have had difficulty with it. Nevertheless, explain it you must, even though you greatly oversimplify it. The most effective way to do so is by concrete example. You might, for example, write something like the following:

> If the standard of care imposed on Busarus was ordinary, then the act of the bus driver in starting up without determining what had happened to Susan when she disappeared from view was not negligent, especially given that a teacher was standing by to supervise the unloading of the bus. However, if a higher standard of care is imposed under the Transit case, then the driver will likely be found negligent, because that standard of care requires . . .

Note that you cannot determine what the jury finding will be, but you can and should indicate what difference a particular standard of care will probably make in the result if the finding is as you expect, given that the standard of care imposed will affect the judge's instruction to the jury.

Considerations of Style

Before starting to write, spend a few minutes thinking about style. In writing an opinion, you are writing not as an advocate, the role you are most accustomed to, but as a lawgiver, an authority, whose opinion will significantly affect the course of action your client may choose. Perhaps you have noticed that the best judges do not allow their role as lawgiver to give their language pomposity, or a false sense of importance. You must carefully avoid the appearance of pomposity, and that is equally true whether your client is a lawyer or not. Take a few minutes to read the section on ways to enhance readability in Part IV. Remember that you are not talking down from the bench but across, on the same level as your reader.

Do not write a sentence like this:

> The court in the *Consolidated* case was clearly wrong, as are the opinions that have followed it. The purpose of the rule in *Jones* has never been clearly understood by the courts or the bar.

You can get the same idea across and avoid vagueness by writing something like this:

> Although the reasoning of the *Consolidated* case has been followed in other cases, some authorities think its application of the rule in *Jones* is incorrect, and they therefore think that *Consolidated* may be overturned.

In your care to avoid wordiness, you should avoid going to the opposite extreme either. We demonstrated the legal brief style of writing in chapter 8, and we noted that it was extremely economical, even to the point of being abrupt and choppy. Here, you are writing a letter, so it ought to flow like any well-written business letter. That means you must not drop into the habit of using all short, "telegraphic" sentences. The essence of good writing style is using sentences of varying length and complexity. Do not make the mistake of thinking that because you are writing to a layperson about a complex legal issue, you must write in short sentences as if you were speaking to a child. That is the only thing you can do that will irritate your client more than using legal jargon and Latin phrases.

Another common mistake, and one you must try to eliminate in your rereading of the letter for clarity and economy of language, is the mistake of allowing your words to reflect the order of your thinking rather than the order in which the reader's thinking must progress. For example, you might write a sentence like this:

> Agency is a relationship requiring a determination of many factors, the most important of which is whether the employee is directed as to the details of performance, or only the result, and, of course, whether there is an employer-employee relationship to begin with.

That sentence reflects how you began thinking about the problem, and it follows your train of thought. As a first draft it is quite acceptable. However, to make it easier for the reader, it ought to be revised into two sentences as follows:

> Courts determine whether an employee stands in the relation of agent or independent contractor to his employer on the basis of whether the employer has the right to direct details of the employee's performance or only the result. The court may consider other factors as well.

What we have done is change the order of words to begin with the first consideration, that there is an employment relationship. We have proceeded from there to consideration of what principally determines the category of employment the case falls into, and finally, we noted that other factors may be considered as well. In the process we have intentionally eliminated the passive voice entirely, an important feature of all forceful writing. (For more on this and related stylistic matters, see chapters 15 and 16.)

Writing an Adverse Opinion

When a client asks you to write an opinion about whether an intended course of action will have any adverse legal consequences (that he or she won't be subject to a civil suit and won't be violating any criminal laws), what the client is often looking for is an insurance policy from you, although he or she will seldom put it so bluntly. The last thing your client wants to hear from you is that he or she cannot follow a specific course of action without incurring some problems. The last thing you want to do is tell the client that everything is going to be all right when you don't think so. If your research indicates the intended course of action is perfectly lawful, you should have no difficulty in writing an opinion, but you will rarely enjoy such unadulterated pleasure in your practice. It is more likely that the proposed activity is questionable, and there is a good chance your client had an inkling of this when he or she asked you for an opinion.

The best thing a lawyer can do in this circumstance is to find and suggest to the client a different and legal way of doing what he or she wants. When you succeed in doing so, you earn your client's admiration and trust, so much so that your client will probably tell friends about what a smart lawyer he or she has. When you aren't able to find a lawful way to do what your client wants after several trials and errors (perhaps you have suggested several alternative procedures and he or she has responded to each with business reasons why he or she cannot use them), you are relieved by circumstances from having to write an opinion. You can simply tell your client that you have not found a lawful way for him or her to proceed with the intended course of action. At this point, if you have been able to suggest one or two alternatives, you have at least earned your client's respect, if not his or her gratitude.

When you have studied the problem your client has presented, and you cannot find any way that the client can accomplish the intended action within the law, you have three alternatives: (1) you can write an opinion that points out the illegality of the client's intended course of action and the penalty imposed for a violation of the law, (2) you can write an approving opinion and hope he or she does not get caught, or (3) you can invite the client to lunch. You have already observed, we hope, that (3) is the only sensible choice. After a delicious lunch at his favorite restaurant, you will show your client the admonitory opinion you have written, and you will suggest that you not send it to him. Your client will naturally agree, and you will take the opinion back to your office and shred it. You will find you have not only kept a client, you have increased your client's trust, and that, after all, is your objective.

Revising an Opinion Letter

As with all your writing tasks, you should revise your work, looking for general issues, such as effective order of presentation. Use the checklist to guide your revision.

Checklist: Writing a Legal Opinion

Audience

If you are writing for a lay client, have you simply explained the key legal issues, defining terminology where necessary?

Tone

1. Have you used a professional, business tone, even if you know the client well?
2. On the other hand, have you avoided pompous language?

Contents

1. Have you recited the relevant facts?
2. Have you stated the law and explained the probable outcome given the facts as they are known?
3. Is your conclusion clearly stated, even if you are stating uncertainty?

Organization

1. Have you included these sections: recitation of the facts, legal analysis, and your opinion or conclusion?
2. Have you placed the legal analysis before your opinion or conclusion if your conclusion is uncertain? Conversely, have you stated your conclusion first if the case is relatively straightforward?

Final Comments

The writing tasks associated with the Ames case are now complete, except for any associated with a possible appeal, and you have participated with us in the process of writing several legal documents as they would occur in handling an actual case. We have demonstrated the strategies and techniques we recommend by examples from a negligence case. But these strategies and techniques apply across all the legal specialties and all the writing tasks. Although a file memorandum is a different product with a different purpose and audience and style from a trial brief, the way you approach each writing task, the way you analyze and select your writing choices is the same for every document and for every kind of matter, whether it is constitutional law, domestic relations, or securities law that you are practicing.

PART III

Conventions for Organizing Documents

CHAPTER 10

How to Write Effective Introductions and Conclusions

Introductions and conclusions are key parts of legal documents: they are what your readers see first and last, and they have the potential of making a positive and forceful impression on your readers.

How to Write Reader-Friendly Introductions

Regardless of whether you are writing an informative office memo, a letter to a client requesting information, or a persuasive brief, your introductions should follow a *CPO format*—that is, they should establish the *context* for the document, clarify the *purpose* for writing the document, and explain the *organization* of the document. The only exception to this convention occurs when your topic is highly controversial or emotional and likely to threaten your readers. When you are faced with this sort of "hot" communication situation, then consider following a less offensive posture, as discussed in chapter 13.

The CPO format works on the principle that you should move from *given information*—that is, what the reader knows—to *new information*—that is, what the reader does not know. According to readability studies, readers and listeners comprehend and recall information better when it is presented in this deductive manner. By establishing the main points of a document before launching into a detailed analysis of these points, you show readers what information to look for. Unlike readers of airport novels, readers of professional and technical documents are not reading for pleasure, and they do not want surprises in the middle or the end of the document.

You can create the context for a document by elaborating on the common ground that you share with your reader. As discussed in the opening chapters to this book, readers will be more sympathetic to your point of view if you account for their knowledge, interests, and level of education. When the significance of the subject is *not* immediately apparent, you need to educate your readers. As a result, you will sometimes need to write several paragraphs or pages outlining the history of a problem and its scope, while other times a simple sentence or even a title will do.

As an example of the importance of a CPO format, consider which of the following two introductions seems stronger:

> **Sample One:** I have spent the last twenty days or so reading the most significant and recent literature and reviewing past notes and materials on the facts, issues, and methodology of establishing appropriate and reasonable compensation for shareholders. Much of the stuff being written these days has the same body and substance dressed in different colored apparel and trappings. I have not found anyone who has developed a particular approach or methodology that could even serve as a primary guide for establishment of an overall mathematical formula.
>
> **Sample Two:** After carefully studying methods to assign salaries for lawyers, I have been unable to find an exact method to ensure appropriate and reasonable compensation for shareholders in our firm. Nevertheless, I have identified five criteria that we should consider: (1) past salary, (2) financial contributions, (3) intangible contributions, (4) cost of living adjustments, (5) and competition with other firms. Below I describe these concerns in detail so that we can be sure to discuss them at our annual shareholders' meeting.

If you are like most readers, you will prefer the latter introduction because it concisely presents the context, purpose, and organization for the document. Most busy readers become annoyed when you keep them guessing about the purpose for a document. Busy readers do not want extensive background information before the significance of the subject is clarified, nor do they want to hear lengthy definitions before they learn the overall problem being considered. Finally, you can aid comprehension by forecasting how you have organized a document. In a sentence, or a few short sentences, give your reader a sense of how the document is organized, as illustrated by the sample below.

> Dear Bill:
>
> This is in reply to your request for an update on our motion to dismiss the Amalgamated amended complaint filed last week. We have not yet filed our motion; and it is not quite complete, but the substance of it is as follows. First, I will give you a summary of the facts Amalgamated is pleading, and then I will summarize the argument that Amalgamated has failed to state a

> cause of action. Finally, I will give you our conclusion as we intend to present it to Judge Madison.

When evaluating how explicit you need to be about how you have organized a document, consider your audience. Highly educated readers require less guidance than less educated ones. Also, if your document is organized according to legal conventions, then lawyers will need fewer transitional sentences than nonlawyers.

How to Write Forceful Conclusions

Many lawyers fail to recognize the importance of conclusions. Even if your introduction forcefully presents the topic or the argument and even if the body of the document is logical and well developed, you still need to pay considerable attention to the conclusion because it provides your last opportunity to emphasize key issues or to be persuasive. Readability studies have suggested that a powerful conclusion is second only to the introduction in terms of its effect on a reader.

Of course, your communication situation defines how much detail you will need to go into in your conclusion. A 200-page document, for example, will place different demands on you than a conclusion to a short letter. In general, conclusions should energetically and concisely summarize the gist of a document. When your purpose is to be persuasive, you may also want to include a few emotional appeals to encourage your readers to take the action or make the decision you want. Before considering your conclusion to be complete, ask the following questions:

1. What are the broad implications of your conclusions? What recommendations can you make based on the material that you have presented?
2. Would it be appropriate for you to speculate on what will happen next?
3. Are there any questions that you want your audience to answer or do you want to invite questions from your readers?
4. Would it be appropriate for you to use emotional appeals to motivate your readers?

CHAPTER 11

How to Shape Paragraphs

Many of the principles that we discussed in the previous chapter for introducing documents are equally applicable at the paragraph level. Your goals for the opening sentences of your paragraphs are similar to your goals when writing an introduction to a long document: you want your beginning sentences to clarify the purpose of the paragraph. Also, many paragraphs move deductively—that is, the first sentence presents the *topic* or *theme* of the paragraph and the following sentences illustrate and explicate this theme.

Unlike punctuation, which is subject to specific rules, we cannot offer ironclad guidelines for shaping paragraphs. If you presented a text without paragraphs to a dozen lawyers and asked them to break the document into logical sections, chances are that you would get twelve different opinions about the best places to put the paragraph breaks. Some of the greatest legal writers have occasionally broken the conventions for shaping paragraphs. Oliver Wendell Holmes, Jr., Benjamin N. Cardozo, Robert H. Jackson, and similarly distinguished legal writers have routinely shaped paragraphs that lack topic sentences, that contain multiple topics, and that extend beyond a single page. When writing, therefore, you should trust your intuition about where to place the paragraphs, and then, when revising, consider the following guidelines as general "rules of thumb."

Deductive Paragraph Organization

Most legal paragraphs follow a deductive organization that moves from given to new information, or from the general to the specific. The first sentence of a deductively organized paragraph is often called the topic sentence because it identifies the theme being considered. Subsequent sentences then restrict or illustrate this theme. To ensure that you have established the logical transitions between sentences in a paragraph that is deductively organized, Francis Christensen, a noted writer on rhetoric, has suggested numbering sentences from most general to most specific. Below is an example of how Christensen would map a paragraph from J. Bronowski's *The Common Sense of Science:*[1]

1. The process of learning is essential to our lives.
    2. All higher animals seek it deliberately.
        3. They are inquisitive and they experiment.
            4. An experiment is a sort of harmless trial run of some action which we shall have to make in the real world; and this, whether it is made in the laboratory by scientists or by fox-cubs outside their earth.
                5. The scientist experiments and the cub plays; both are learning to correct their errors of judgment in a setting in which errors are not fatal.
                    6. Perhaps this is what gives them both their air of happiness and freedom in these activities.

Of course, Christensen is *not* suggesting that all paragraphs should be shaped deductively. By studying the works of professionals, he also notes that some paragraphs are shaped in a coordinate way and others in an inductive way. Below is a sample of coordinate pattern, which Christensen took from Bergen Evans's *Comfortable Words:*[2]

1. He [the native speaker] may, of course, speak a form of English that marks him as coming from a rural or an unread group.
    2. But if he doesn't mind being so marked, there's no reason why he should change.
        3. Samuel Johnson kept a Staffordshire burr in his speech all his life.
        3. In Burns's mouth, the despised lowland Scots dialect served just as well as the "correct" English spoken by ten million of his southern contemporaries.

1. Francis Christensen, *Notes Toward a New Rhetoric* (New York: Harper & Row, 1967), 60.
2. Christensen, 63.

3. Lincoln's vocabulary and his way of pronouncing certain words were sneered at by many better educated people at the time, but he seemed to be able to use the English language as effectively as his critics.

Inductive Paragraph Structure

Because readers of legal writing generally expect writers to proceed from the *given* to the *new,* they have little patience for *inductive paragraphs*—that is, paragraphs that move logically from the particular to the general. However, an inductive structure can occasionally be appropriate for an audience interested in analyzing principles of law, for dramatic conclusions, or for a varied style.

For example, when you are writing to audiences who are interested in the principles of law or when you are bringing up information that is likely to antagonize your audience, you may wish to have an inductive opening. The following excerpt, which is also from *Palsgraf v. Long Island,* illustrates how an accomplished writer uses an inductive and chronological review of the facts to help readers visualize the accident scene. Rather than giving readers the reason for the review of the accident scene—that a plaintiff is seeking damages for her injuries—Cardozo opens his argument with all of the trappings of a good suspense novel: in chronological order, he describes how the accident occurred. It is not until the last sentence of the paragraph that he explains why he has so reviewed the particulars of the accident scene:

> CARDOZO, C.J. Plaintiff was standing on a platform of the defendant's railroad after buying a ticket to go to Rockaway Beach. A train stopped at the station, bound for another place. Two men ran forward to catch it. One of the men reached the platform of the car without mishap, though the train was already moving. The other man, carrying a package, jumped aboard the car but seemed unsteady as if about to fall. A guard on the car, who had held the door open, reached forward to help him in, and another guard on the platform pushed him from behind. In this act, the package was dislodged and fell on the rails. It was a package of small size, about fifteen inches long, and was covered by a newspaper. In fact it contained fireworks, but there was nothing in its appearance to give notice of its contents. The fireworks, when the man fell, exploded. The shock of the explosion threw down some scales at the other end of the platform many feet away. The scales struck the plaintiff, causing injuries for which she sues.

Keeping Paragraphs to One Specific Purpose or Theme

Regardless of whether a paragraph is shaped in a deductive, coordinate, or inductive way, it should be unified by a single purpose. When you fail to discuss the central idea identified in the topic sentence or when you mix ideas in a single paragraph, you can confuse readers because you are violating their sense of order. In the following sample passage, for example, the first sentence sets the stage for an argument that analyzes the application of the standard of *reckless* from *Hackbart v. Holmes* (675 F2d 1114, 1118 (10th Circ. 19832)) to the current case in a separate paragraph being argued. More specifically, the introductory sentence leads readers to believe that the paragraph will demonstrate that the court requires more than "careless, inattentive or grossly negligent" to apply the reckless standard and that the facts of the current case do not warrant such an application. Unfortunately, however, the promise implied by this opening sentence is never fulfilled, as the bulk of the paragraph simply reviews *Hackbart* without linking it to the current case. Finally, note how the last sentence introduces an altogether new idea, which should be developed and related to the current case if it is mentioned:

> The defendant submits that a study of *Hackbart* indicates that in this circuit more than "careless, inattentive or grossly negligent" is required to meet the standard of reckless, so the court could therefore find that the defendant did not engage in reckless conduct. The seller or defendant in *Hackbart* knew what he was doing or it was so obvious that he was aware of what he was doing. According to the court's finding, the plaintiff or purchaser was naive and could have reasonably trusted his friend of some thirty years. Even in view of that relationship, the defendant went ahead with a scheme whereby he had his lawyer propose a plan for the purchaser which was much different than his earlier proposal. Clearly, the defendant engaged in intentional practices and at the very least should have under the circumstances done his very best to assure that the purchaser understood the change in the arrangement. Also, the defendant benefited financially from the scheme.

Establishing Logical Transitions Between Ideas

Like branches that extend gracefully from an old oak tree, paragraphs must relate to each other as well as the overall purpose of a text. The order in which you place your paragraphs is determined by the logic of your argument or by the chronology of events that you are reviewing. As a result, you can best establish coherence among paragraphs by following the most logical inherent order.

Establishing transitional sentences for paragraphs is often the most difficult challenge you face as a writer because you need to guide the reader with a light hand. When you are too blatant about transitions, your readers may feel patronized. To highlight the connections between your ideas, some stylists suggest providing transitional sentences at the end of each paragraph that look forward to the substance of the next paragraph. While we agree that you may *occasionally* want to do this, we also warn that too many *explicit* transitional sentences and phrases can appear obtrusive, thereby undercutting your credibility. At best, readers perceive too many explicit transitions to be wordy; at worst, they perceive the sentences as insulting. After all, they imply that you, the reader, are too inept to follow the discussion. When scanning the following introductory paragraph on lawyers' salaries, do you feel as if you are stuck behind an unbearably long red light at a traffic intersection? Do you find yourself screaming to yourself, "Get to the point!"

> What I hope to do in this memo is to set out some of the major elements that, in my judgment, should be considered by the Committee in establishing shareholder compensation. Let me turn, then, to the more specific indices which the Firm may wish to consider in setting compensation. . . . As with the general factors set above, the more specific elements may not be fully comprehensive, although I have attempted to make them so. The more discrete factors which will ordinarily yield strong and reliable data are addressed in the following paragraphs.

We also encourage you to take a hard look at the frequency of transitional phrases that you employ. *Again, besides, equally important, furthermore, however, in contrast, on the other hand, meanwhile, for example, as noted, in brief*—these sorts of transitional words can be helpful when used occasionally. When used excessively, however, they create a choppy, obtrusive, listlike style. Finally, note that words like *therefore, consequently, thus, as a result,* and *hence* cannot in themselves provide logical connections if the ideas they connect do not flow logically together.

Varying the Length of Paragraphs

Different ideas, arguments, and chronologies warrant their own paragraph lengths, so the form of your text should emerge in response to your thoughts. When evaluating how you have structured your ideas, however, pay some attention to whether you have varied the length of your paragraphs. Short paragraphs tend to create a listlike style, which intrudes on clarity and persuasive appeal. Notice when you read the following, for example, that short paragraphs make you work harder to understand the writer's message (although convention dictates that pleadings be written this way):

> For claims against the defendants, plaintiff alleges as follows:
> First Claim for Relief
>
> 1. Plaintiff, at all times herein mentioned, owned the premises consisting of the upstairs and downstairs apartment and storage unit located at 1436 St. on Cowboy Lane, Austin, Texas.
> 2. On or before March 15, 1981, plaintiff leased to defendants, George Nelson and Susan Nelson, an upstairs apartment at 1436 St. on Cowboy Lane, Austin, Texas for $185.00
> 3. By virtue of said agreements, defendants went into possession of said premises, and ever since have held and still continue to hold possession or control of said premises as tenants of the plaintiff and are responsible for rent payments as per their agreement.
> 4. Pursuant to the terms of the agreement, there became due and owing from defendants to plaintiff rent which remains unpaid for the use of said premises in the sum of $5,285 through January 1, 1992.

Just as short paragraphs can render the simple complicated, long paragraphs can seem impenetrable to the weary eye. Thus, you should ask yourself whether you can introduce a short paragraph of two or three sentences between longer ones to give your readers a break and to make your document more visually appealing.

Different Types of Paragraphs

There are four common patterns of paragraph development. The advantage of using these paragraph patterns is that your readers are accustomed to them. Understandably, however, you will occasionally want to develop other ways to organize paragraphs.

THE TRANSITIONAL PARAGRAPH

As we discussed earlier, readers appreciate your establishing the context, purpose, and organization of your document in the opening paragraphs. By making forecasting statements, you help your readers understand how new information relates to given information.

When your readers are trudging through the body of a rather complicated document, they want reminders about how each subsection relates to the argument or discussion as a whole. When you are addressing a highly technical or complicated subject, you will want to routinely review your discussion or argument up to that point and forecast new directions in your thinking. Essentially, then, you need to provide mini-introductions throughout your texts to serve as reminders to your readers about why they are being given the information and how it relates to the overall purpose that drives the document. Of course, you can also highlight transitions from one subject to another by using headings, subheadings, and numbers.

When a case is relevant to several of the issues that you are analyzing, you should elaborate on the case for each issue. In other words, you should not presume that your readers will make the necessary connection between your case and another case's holding in relation to issue B just because it is logical to do so given that you elaborated on the case's holding when discussing issue A. However, you should avoid giving the impression that you are patronizing the reader. If your discussion of case X occurred only a few paragraphs ago, for example, you would not need to elaborate verbatim and in equal detail on how it supports issue C. Instead, you can briefly refer to the earlier discussion and its current significance to issue C.

THE ARGUMENTATIVE/IRAC PARAGRAPH

Most arguments require more than a paragraph for complete development. Yet one of your minor claims may fit nicely into a paragraph. For instance, a paragraph could begin with a claim about how a rule of law applies to a fact situation. Readers would then expect you to elaborate on the law and its relationship to the facts of the case. This is the IRAC approach: Issue, Rule, Application, Conclusion. See chapter 9 for a fuller discussion of this approach to legal argument.

Incidentally, when revising, you should evaluate a paragraph-length argument with the same rigor with which you attack arguments at the textual level: each claim should have sufficient supporting evidence, and the way in which the data supports the claim needs to be made clear.

THE PROBLEM-SOLUTION PARAGRAPH

When you begin a paragraph with a question, your readers expect the paragraph (and perhaps a few others) to work at answering this question. If you followed a sentence such as, "How can we ensure that the youngest members in the firm receive compensation for their workloads?" your readers would expect the paragraph, and perhaps subsequent paragraphs, to tackle this issue.

THE CHRONOLOGICAL-ORDER PARAGRAPH

Phrases like "The first step in . . ." or "Our concerns focus on three major events . . ." immediately cue readers that a chronology will follow. Note, for example, how the following sentence leads you to anticipate a chronological narration of the events: "We have four major events that occurred on consecutive days, thus establishing a pattern of behavior . . ."

CHAPTER 12

How to Organize the Body of Expository Documents

As a lawyer, much of your time involves *analyzing* problems and concepts. For example, you routinely analyze how the law applies to given situations. To do this, you break a problem down into numerous issues by asking questions, such as these: What are the main parts of the problem? What specific questions or issues are most important? How are these events related to each other? Can they be organized in chronological fashion? Do they imply a cause-and-effect relationship?

Sometimes your communication situation dictates how a document should be organized. When you are writing a reply brief, for example, you will usually want to follow the order of issues that the opposing counsel has forced you to consider. In addition, the conventions of law often dictate how you structure documents. For example, Rule 28 of the Federal Rules of Appellate Procedure requires an appellant's brief to contain five elements: a table of contents, an issues section, a statement of the case section, an argument section, and a conclusion section.

When external factors do not require a specific organization, you can determine how to best organize your manuscripts by noting the primary question or questions that you are asking. When your primary purpose for writing is to answer the question "What problem or concept am I defining?" you are writing a *subject* or *topic analysis*. In turn, when you are answering "How did this process evolve?" "What is the history of this particular legal problem?" or "How is this done?" you are writing a *process analysis*. Finally, when asking "What is the effect of this?" or "Why did this happen?" you are writing a *causal analysis*—that is, a document that explores a cause-and-effect relationship.

Of course, most legal documents contain elements of subject, process, and causal analyses. It is fairly routine, for instance, for a report that is written to explain *why* something happened, to also define *what* the subject is, *what* factors led up to the event, and *how* the different factors influenced each other to lead up to the event. For instance, in the case study presented in Part II, we were considering *what* damages were done to the plaintiff, *how* the accident happened, *how* it could have been avoided, and *why* we could anticipate additional pain and suffering on the plaintiff's part.

This overlapping among subject, process and causal analyses is not surprising when you realize that analysis is fundamental to all forms of knowing and writing. At the most elementary level, all writing involves analyzing and reporting information; all thinking begins by questioning and analyzing information. Nevertheless, as we demonstrate below, identifying what is your dominant purpose for writing can help you better organize your work.

Subject Analysis

Many legal documents are organized according to the order of significance of the issues to the overall concept or problem. When this is the case, you need to order the issues in their order of importance and then explicate them, as illustrated in the sample outline.

Outline for a Subject Analysis

1. Provide a CPO introduction (see chapter 9). Explain the criteria you have used to define the problem or concept. Give an overview of the major parts of the problem.
2. Discuss subissue #1. Explain its significance to the problem.
3. Discuss subissue #2. Explain its significance to the problem. Continue in this manner until all subissues are defined.
4. Once each issue has been discussed separately, analyze how the issues are interconnected.
5. Provide a forceful conclusion (see chapter 9).

It is also common to organize a document according to the authority of the forms of law you cite. Generally speaking, you should address constitutional questions before statutory questions or common law questions.

Process Analysis

You will occasionally need to explain the evolution of judicial doctrine or explain how a legal problem occurred. To ensure communication, you can number the important steps in the process that you are describing. You can also use transitional words to help cue the reader about different steps in the process, such as *first, second, next, then, now, at this point.* For long and detailed processes, you may want to include a flowchart—that is, a visual representation of the subject. If you do so, remember to introduce the flowchart early in the document so readers can refer to it as they read the document.

Organizing documents by chronological order is much simpler than organizing by subject priority. After all, as indicated by the sample outline, all you need to do is establish the correct order of events to organize your work.

Outline for a Process Analysis

1. Provide a CPO introduction.
2. If describing a complicated process, offer a flowchart.
3. Describe step or event 1.
4. Describe step or event 2.
5. Describe step or event 3 and subsequent steps.
6. Provide a forceful conclusion.

Causal Analysis

Exploring cause-and-effect relationships is among the most difficult writing lawyers do. When analyzing causal relationships, you must question how different parts and sequences interact with each other over time. Rather than merely reporting the order of events in chronological fashion as you do when describing a process, you need to identify the specific reasons behind the effects. This is often difficult because a single cause can result in many different effects and an effect can have multiple causes. When analyzing what causes led to an effect, question whether you have identified all of the *necessary* and *sufficient* causes. For example, in order to have a fire (effect), you need three causes: combustible material, oxygen, and ignition temperature. Without these three necessary causes working in tandem, you do not have a sufficient explanation of the effect.

Explanations of causes can be even more problematical. No simple solutions can be provided, for example, to explain why some people become violent criminals. As you know from your practice, attempts to explain human behavior are far more difficult than explaining how physical phenomena interact in a laboratory. Even after exhausting all of the potential causes for an action and organizing them into *primary* and *secondary causes,* you often still need to soften your claim of causality by using words like *may, often, sometimes* or *most.* When drafting a document that explores a cause-and-effect relationship, consider the sample outline.

Outline for a Causal Analysis

Explaining Effects

1. Provide a CPO introduction.
2. Explain whether the effect can be linked to a single cause or to a serious of causes that work in sequence or simultaneously.
3. Elaborate on the first, second, and third causes of the effect.
4. Consider counterarguments: Could other unrelated causes explain this effect?
5. Could an action have been taken or a situation changed to avoid the effect?
6. Provide a forceful conclusion.

Analyzing Causes

1. Provide a CPO introduction.
2. Analyze the cause.
3. Elaborate on the first, second, and third effects of the cause.
4. Consider counterarguments: Could other unrelated effects result from this cause?
5. Could an action have been taken or a situation changed to avoid the cause?
6. Provide a forceful conclusion.

When explaining effects or causes, you need to avoid making a *post hoc fallacy,* which means that you should avoid assuming a cause-and-effect relationship when one event may simply have occurred after another without being caused by it. A *post hoc* fallacy occurs when someone assumes event B was caused by event A because it occurred after event A when it is also possible that event B was caused by some other factor. For example, if your client dies of cancer, you need to establish not merely that he or she came in contact with possible cancer-causing chemicals, but that the cancer was not likely to have been caused by anything else, such as cigarette smoking.

CHAPTER 13

How to Organize the Body of Persuasive Documents

In this chapter, we present two dramatically different ways to organize winning arguments. The first organizational structure, which can be traced to the writings of Aristotle, is appropriate when your audience includes judges and juries. The second organizational scheme, which developed out of the client-centered therapy advocated by Carl Rogers, is more appropriate when you are willing to compromise and are attempting to establish some consensus between opposing positions.[1]

Traditional Persuasion

There is, of course, no single ideal way to structure an argument. You should, nonetheless, consider whether the following organizing strategies can help you make your ideas more accessible to readers.

The outline on the next page summarizes a traditional way of organizing a persuasive argument.

1. However, the form of "soft negotiation" that we recommend is not a true depiction of what rhetoricians call "Rogerian Persuasion" because we do not ask you to challenge yourself to risk change. If you were truly engaged in a Rogerian approach, then you would need to be so open-minded that you entertained the possibility that you are misguided in your beliefs. According to Rogers, you must "run the risk of being changed yourself. You . . . might find yourself influenced in your attitudes or your personality." Taken to the extreme, the Rogerian approach would even have you reconsider your position, which, of course, is a "pipe dream" in most legal writing situations.

Outline for Traditional Persuasion

1. Provide a CPO introduction.
2. Establish ethical appeals.
3. State your claim.
4. Present counterarguments.
5. Establish emotional appeals, if appropriate.
6. Provide a forceful conclusion.

TYPES OF APPEALS

By examining the insights of other thinkers and the strategies that the people of his day employed to sway opinion, Aristotle described three kinds of appeals that speech makers of his day commonly made: *ethical (ethos) appeals, logical (logos) appeals,* and *emotional (pathos) appeals.*

The term *ethical appeal* refers to the *voice* or *persona* that writers project, and this term should not be confused with "ethics."[2] As you know, some people are particularly gifted at projecting a trusting, friendly persona when their ultimate goal is to take advantage of your goodwill or an oversight on your part. According to the traditional model of persuasion, appeals based on *ethos* are most powerful when placed in the introductory and concluding paragraphs of your documents.

Despite the forcefulness of ethical appeals, you need to use *logical appeals* if you hope to sway educated readers. Your readers will expect you to provide evidence—that is, logical reasoning, expert testimony, facts, and statistics. Successful lawyers pride themselves on overcoming social and emotional appeals by logic.

While *emotional appeals* are inappropriate in many legal situations, you may want to use them when addressing a jury or clients. After all, we tend to perceive situations subjectively and passionately—particularly situations that involve us at a personal level or that are controversial. Even when we try to be objective, many of us still make decisions based on emotional impulses rather than sound reasoning. Like ethical appeals, however, emotional appeals lack persuasion when overemphasized. Most modern readers—particularly well educated ones—are quick to see through such manipulative attempts. According to the tenets of traditional persuasion, therefore, you are advised to provide emotional appeals *after* you have provided sufficient logical support.

---

2. For a more complete discussion of how to establish an effective persona, see chapter 1, pp. 10-11.

STATEMENT OF CLAIM

Once you have educated your reader about the complexity of the problem that you are addressing, you should consider explicitly mentioning the claim about your position.

PRESENTING COUNTERARGUMENTS

At some point in your document—most commonly in the introduction or near the conclusion—you will need to present likely counterarguments to your claim. After all, the opposition will have its own rules and cases to cite. To ignore the counterarguments is to ignore reality. Essentially, whenever you think your readers are likely to disagree with you, you need to account for their concerns. Elaborating on counterarguments is particularly useful when you have an unusual claim or when you believe your audience may be more inclined to perceive a different claim as more valid.

However, please note that you will sabotage your hard-won persona as an informed and fair-minded thinker if you misrepresent your opponent's counterarguments. When presenting your opponent's views, remember that your readers do not expect your position to be valid 100 percent of the time. Few people think so simplistically, and few subjects that are worth arguing about can be reduced to *yes* or *no*. When pertinent, therefore, you should concede those instances in which your opponents are right about their position, while still arriving at the conclusion that you are right.

One tactic that judges and other skilled critical readers dislike is the *straw-man approach*, which occurs when an author misrepresents an opponent's argument or presents a weak aspect of the opponent's argument as representative of the strength of the argument as a whole. Before presenting a *straw-man approach*, you should remember that misrepresenting or deliberately understating an opponent's arguments about the subject may turn thoughtful readers against you instead of enabling you to carry the day.

Soft Negotiation

When writing to a trial court or an appellant court, you face what rhetoricians call a *triadic communication situation*. Essentially, this means that a third party (that is, a judge) will decide which of two arguments is most convincing. In such situations you are wise to state the facts of the case and pertinent law in your introductory remarks. In short, you can come out shooting and try to win the argument through logic, reason, and, perhaps, a pinch of emotion.

However, when you face a *dyadic communication situation*—that is, when your audience *is* the opposition—then you may want to choose a more diplomatic way to structure your argument. Instead of assuming that you should attempt to overcome an antagonistic audience with shrewd reasoning, the goal of soft negotiation is to establish common ground for communication and then work out a compromise agreement. Your goal when you employ the tactics of soft negotiation is not for you to win and for your opponent to lose—a scenario that more often results in both parties losing. Instead, your goal centers around exploring ways that will allow both you and your audience to win.

When you are addressing a complicated or emotional topic, one that will threaten the values and assumptions of the primary audience for the document, you may want to consider an alternative to traditional persuasion like the one in the outline.

Outline for Soft Negotiation

1. Present the problem that needs to be solved.
2. Elaborate on the value of opposing positions.
3. Present your claim in a nonthreatening way; show instances when your opinions are valid.
4. Search for a compromise and call for a higher interest.

PRESENTING THE PROBLEM THAT NEEDS TO BE SOLVED

In the introduction of your document, identify the issue and clarify its significance. Because you need to adopt a nonthreatening persona throughout your document, however, avoid dogmatically presenting your view as the best or only way to solve the problem. Unlike traditional argument, at this point in your discussion you will *not* want to lay your cards down on the table and summarize the gist of your opinion. Instead, you should present the problem as a complicated one that can best be solved by finding as much consensus as possible between the various viewpoints.

ELABORATING ON THE VALUE OF OPPOSING POSITIONS

In this part of your argument, you may want to elaborate on the instances in which your opponent's claims about the problem are correct. In your introduction and throughout your persuasive documents, you will want to explain the problem in ways so that your audience feels, "Yes, this author understands my position." Because the people to whom you are writing may feel antagonistic when you confront them with an emotionally charged issue about which they disagree with you, they will seek every possible way to avoid reading (or listening to) you. Since they have already made up their mind on the subject and are especially reluctant readers, you should try to interest them by suggesting that you have an innovative way of viewing the problem. Of course, this tactic is only effective when you can indeed follow through and be original in your treatment of the subject. Otherwise your readers may reject your ideas because they may feel you have misrepresented yourself.

PRESENTING YOUR CLAIMS IN A NONTHREATENING WAY

Once you have identified the problem in as nonthreatening a way as possible, established a fair-minded persona, and perhaps called for some level of consensus based on a higher interest, you have reached the most important stage in soft negotiation: you can now present your position. At this point in your argument, however, you do not want to slap down a *But!* or *However!* and then come out of your corner punching.

It is difficult to substantiate your argument while still appeasing your antagonistic audience, yet if you have done an effective job in the early part of your document (or speech), then your audience will now perceive you to be a reasonable person—someone well worth listening to. Consequently, you should not sell yourself short when presenting your position.

To achieve the nonthreatening tone needed to defuse emotional situations, avoid exaggerating your claims or using biased, emotional language. Also, avoid attacking your audience's exaggerated claims. Whenever you feel angry or defensive, take a deep breath and look for points in which you can agree with your opponents' claims. When you are really angry about an issue, you may find it extraordinarily difficult to cool off enough to recognize that your language is loaded with contentious terms.

Because of the emotionally charged context of your communication situation, however, you still need to maintain the same open-minded persona that you began your document with. Although your main focus in this section is to develop the validity of your claim, you can still ensure your fair-minded persona by recalling significant counterarguments and by elaborating on a few limitations with your claim. You can also remind your readers that you are not expecting them to completely accept your claim. Instead, you are merely attempting to show that under certain circumstances your position is valid.

SEARCHING FOR A COMPROMISE

Near the conclusion of your argument, you should identify a reasonable compromise, one which truly concedes points on both sides of the issue. At this time, you may wish to identify any *higher interests* that you share with your audience.

PART IV

The Doubting Game: Revising and Editing

CHAPTER 14

Jargon and the Plain English Movement

Before discussing revising strategies in the next chapters, we must tackle a sticky question: What is effective legal language? In response, we must admit that there is no single answer. We have few absolute rules on which we can agree. For instance, we can agree that subjects should agree in number with their verbs. Unsure of how to spell a word, we can all open our spell-check programs on our word processing programs or reach for a dictionary. Yet many—if not most—of the decisions that we make as writers do not fall within the boundaries of these *absolute rules.* Instead, we are often working in a shady area of *subjective opinion.*

The Subjective Nature of "Good Writing"

People tend to disagree about what is good writing. Yes, well educated people routinely agree that effective legal language is persuasive, logical, succinct, precise, and well organized. Yet once you give these people a document to read and ask them whether or not it possesses these features, you are likely to find more disagreement than agreement. Certainly, our nation's 800,000 lawyers have more than one idea about what constitutes effective discourse. What one reader calls economical prose, another calls wordy. In fact, even a seemingly innocuous recommendation such as "Good writing is concise" can be contradicted once we consider it in light of a particular communication situation. For example, if you were writing a letter to a client whose daughter had been killed by a drunken driver in a car accident, you would want to go beyond one sentence that said, "I do not recommend that we pursue an appeal of Mr. Henson's not guilty verdict, because the police failed to do a breath analyzer at the scene of the accident." Although such a sentence concisely summarizes your conclusion, it lacks the compassion that you would want to communicate in such an unfortunate circumstance. Even though additional sentences could be perceived as redundant, you probably would still want to talk about previous cases that addressed similar circumstances. Perhaps you also might want to provide the phone numbers of support groups of victims of violent crimes.

Some lawyers even believe that writing poorly is in their best economic interests. Others believe they need to write with the passive voice and punctuate each claim with ponderous case references to sound like a lawyer. Of course, we would be the first to admit that you may occasionally confront a communication situation in which you need to obfuscate your meaning. Your best bet to win a bad case may well be to confuse the judge or jury, so you may someday face a communication situation that requires you to draft vague documents. For example, when legislators cannot develop consensus on an issue with their colleagues, they sometimes "water down" the document so that opposing factions will agree to sign it. Unfortunately, the end result of this process can be a regulation that no one understands and which will require litigation. Although situations where vague writing serves your purpose are rare, you will occasionally face them in your daily practice.

Despite the subjective nature of what makes good writing, *soft rules* do exist that you can consult when evaluating your own and other people's documents. As writers, we are not stranded in a twilight zone where no rules exist, nor are we venturing "where no one has gone before." Instead, we are guided by convention—by how past writers have shaped ideas. Thanks to the recent work of cognitive psychologists and readability experts, we also are guided by an understanding of how different organizational patterns and sentence structures affect a reader's short-term memory. Taken as a whole, these *soft rules* (which are sometimes called *stylistic guidelines* or *readability guidelines*) form the foundation of the *plain English movement.* Some of these rules are discussed in chapters 15 and 16.

The Plain English Movement and the Legal Profession

What started as a group of renegade business leaders and lawyers arguing for plain English quickly burgeoned into a major movement. Ever since the 1970s, when President Carter pushed for "plain English" federal regulations, state legislatures and consumer groups have called for clarity in written documents. By 1980, over half of the states had introduced laws and administrative regulations designed to ensure the readability of legal documents. The impetus empowering this movement is not that lawyers should be prevented from using a reasonable amount of jargon when writing to each other. Most authorities view jargon as an inevitable and profitable way to abbreviate communication among specialists. Instead, the idea behind it is that laypeople have a *right to understand* insurance policies, leases, warranties, tax forms, and other legal documents. Advocates of plain English argue that the gobbledygook and bureaucratese in legal documents are an obstruction of justice because "lawyers themselves cannot agree on the meaning of what they have written."[1] Scarcely a day now goes by without some governmental agency requiring that documents adhere more closely to the standards of plain English.

Admittedly, the reception within the legal community regarding plain English has been mixed. Some senior partners are unaware of, or resistant to, the changes that have occurred in legal language as a result of the plain English movement. Senior partners sometimes go through the memos of junior associates and transform the active voice into the passive (for example, changing "I believe you should do this . . ." to "It is generally recommended that the following actions be instituted . . ."). They add unnecessary Latinisms *(prima facie, res judicata, mens rea)*, awkward legal prepositions (such as *pursuant to*), vague and unnecessary legal terms, unnecessary language from statutes, and archaic words and phrases *(witnesseth, aforesaid, writ, heretofore)*. In our combative and litigious world, it is understandable that many firms are reluctant to change boilerplate that has withstood litigation and the test of time, even if they recognize that the boilerplate is poorly written.

And it is also true that complaints about legal writing are not a new phenomenon. For example, in 1936, Fred Rodell, a professor of law at Harvard, argued that "[t]here are two things wrong with almost all legal writing. One is its style. The other is its content. That, I think, about covers the ground."[2] In Jonathan Swift's well-known satire *Gulliver's Travels*, he attacked lawyers for disguising truth: "There was a society of men among us, bred up from their youth in the art of proving by words multiplied for the purpose, that white is black and black is white, according as they are paid."

Within the last decade, however, lawyers are under more pressure than ever before to make their writing more understandable. These days, you can hardly open up a newspaper or professional journal

1. James Reynolds, "Legal Writing: An Obstruction of Justice," 30 *Alabama Law Review* 1 (Fall 1978).

2. Fred Rodell, "Goodbye to the Law Reviews," 38 *Va. L. Review* (1936).

without seeing an article about some judge, lawyer, or layperson bitterly complaining about poor legal writing. Judges complain about excessive and useless footnoting and about lengthy, poorly argued briefs. Lawyers complain that they cannot understand other lawyers' written documents. For example, John M. Lindsey, a Professor of Law at Temple University School of Law, suggests that

> [t]he current legal writing reformers undoubtedly do good, especially those who try to help lawyers avoid writing like a lawyer. Some, however, may miss the target altogether because they fail to realize that lawyers are being continually exposed to law books, the largest body of poorly written literature ever created by the human race.

In their national survey of 300 lawyers, Professor Jethro Lieberman of New York Law School and Tom Goldstein of the University of California at Berkeley found that most of the 300 lawyers and legal journalists that they surveyed believe that lawyers write poorly.

The bottom line is that lawyers are more determined than ever to write well. Nowadays, clients want to know what they are signing, and they use your writing as a yardstick by which to measure your competence. With more competition among lawyers, members of the legal community are obligated to write concise, precise, and persuasive documents.

In the next two chapters, therefore, we explore this realm of *soft rules*, so that you can ensure that your documents clearly communicate your intentions. Once you are through with chapters 15, 16 and 17, you will have mastered more than two dozen substantive ways to revise and copyedit your documents. As you review your documents to ensure that they are written well, we suggest that you consider these strategies in the order that they are presented, but we also understand that you may want to focus more specifically on one or two of these strategies.

CHAPTER 15

Strategies for Revising Documents

Few lawyers are strangers to revision. From experience, you know that revision involves rereading your work with the eyes of your antagonist. You know that some of your best ideas occur during the revision process and that sometimes you need to discard substantial chunks of your manuscript. As the playwright Neil Simon once remarked, "In baseball, you get only three swings and you're out. In rewriting, you get almost as many swings as you want and you know that, sooner or later, you'll hit the ball."

However, as a lawyer, you do not have all day to stand at the plate and hope to get lucky. Therefore, this chapter explains how you can systematize the revision process so that you can avoid wasted time.

The Nature of the Revising Process

Some lawyers wrongly confuse revising with editing. Revision is *not* a simple matter of correcting the spelling of a few words or copy-editing for grammatical and mechanical correctness. Instead, revision involves making *substantive changes*—global changes that account for fresh insights about what should be said and how the document should be organized. Rather than viewing revision as a form of housekeeping in which you polish the furniture and clean up the clutter, you should perceive revision to be major renovation in which you tear down walls, raise the roof, put windows in to give light to dark rooms, or forcefully demolish the entire structure to make room for a superior home. Unless the matter is routine, you should expect to toss paragraphs around, experiment with new beginnings, chase down new thoughts and feelings, and even discard the first ten pages of an eleven-page document. True revision involves asking, "So what?" and "Who cares?" and looking for cracks and crannies, places where you need to develop or clarify your thinking.

For most writers, revision is the key to success. Writing that reads easily, as if the author were sitting with you and thoroughly and calmly explaining his or her position, is often the product of multiple drafts. When difficult subjects are explained simply, you can assume that the author has agonized over them.

Incidentally, making numerous revisions is *not* necessarily more time consuming than trying to write a perfect first draft. If you freewrite quick first and second drafts and then skim through these notes for the good passages, you can avoid the wasted time and the frustration involved in trying to imagine in your mind how paragraphs will fall or how they will relate to each other.

If you mistake editing for revision, then your first drafts may tyrannize your thinking. Focusing on editorial concerns too soon in the composing process can intrude with your ability to develop ideas. Expecting yourself to write nearly perfect first drafts is like burying yourself in concrete and then trying to beat an opponent in a game of full-court basketball.

Because schools often fail to teach students to revise, however, many lawyers are unaware of the importance of revision. After all, we rarely see the clutter and chaos that led up to the final draft in the published materials that we read. On a daily basis we are bombarded by prose, yet we do not see all of the drafts that contributed to the final production of the document. Unless we know the authors or unless they have been interviewed, we never hear about who helped them develop and polish their documents. As an example of how thoughts become clarified through revision and wording improved, consider the changes that Benjamin Franklin, John Adams, and other committee members appointed to draft a document to explain the colonies' reasons for breaking from England made to Thomas Jefferson's rough draft of the opening sentences of the Declaration of Independence:

> When in the course of human events it becomes necessary for ~~a~~ ^*one* people to
>
> *dissolve the political bands which have connected them with another, and to*
>
> ^ ~~advance from that subordination in which they have hitherto remained, & to~~
>
> assume among the powers of the earth the ^*separate and equal* ~~equal & independent~~ station
>
> to which the laws of nature & of nature's god entitle them, a decent respect

to the opinions of mankind requires that they should declare the causes
the separation.
which impel them to ^ ~~the change~~.

self-evident
We hold these truths to be ~~sacred & undeniable~~: that all men are
they are endowed by their creator with certain
created equal ~~& independent~~; that^ ~~from that equal creationthey derive~~
rights: that *these*
~~in rights inherent &~~ inalienable ^ among ~~which~~ ^ are ~~the preservation of~~

life, ~~&~~ liberty, & the pursuit of happiness. . . .

Below is a final draft of the Declaration of Independence:

> When in the Course of human events, it becomes necessary for one people to dissolve the political bands which have connected them with another, and to assume among the powers of the earth the separate and equal station to which the Laws of Nature and of Nature's God entitle them, a decent respect to the opinions of mankind requires that they should declare the causes which impel them to the separation.
>
> We hold these truths to be self-evident: that all men are created equal; that they are endowed by their Creator with certain unalienable Rights: that among these are Life, Liberty, and the pursuit of Happiness.

Although at first it may seem admirable to ask every critical question that occurs to you when reviewing a rough draft, this is usually a counterproductive approach. Instead, we encourage you to rank order your concerns from most important to least important. For example, if your draft is a rough listing of some incomplete ideas, then you should focus on substantive, global questions, such as these: For whom am I writing? What is my purpose? What persona do I wish to project?

When revising a rough draft, don't fret over grammatical or mechanical questions. After all, you may very well throw out the bulk of your first and second drafts, so there's no sense in taking time to edit these drafts to conform to grammatical conventions.

Because we have ranked the following revising techniques in their order of importance, we suggest that you read and experiment with them in the order that they are presented. Of course, once you are familiar with these critical approaches, you can skip around and use those that seem most appropriate. The checklist at the end of this chapter summarizes the main points to consider as you revise.

Adopting an Aggressive, Fault-finding Attitude

To be successful at revision, you must be willing to attack your thinking. Finding major problems with your logic or presentation, recognizing that you have not accounted for your audience's attitude about the subject, observing redundant passages—these revising activities must be perceived as inevitable and natural occurrences. To be thoroughly successful as a writer, you must be willing to read your work as if it were written by someone else—perhaps even by your worst "enemy."

Allowing Incubation Time Before Revising

Given your busy schedule, our suggestion that you take as much time as possible between revisions may seem unrealistic. Yes, we are sympathetic to the hefty work load that you and other modern lawyers face, and we do know that your firm may put out several thousand pages a day. Yet we also know that most people find it impossible to thoroughly critique a draft shortly after they have written it. Understandably, we all need some distance from our ideas and written drafts before we gain the necessary perspective that will enable us to critique and develop them. It generally makes sense, therefore, that you learn to juggle your writing tasks. By putting document A aside and working on document B before trying to revise document A, you are better prepared to play the role of the opposing lawyer and wedge open any cracks in your reasoning. Even a 15-minute break can be helpful.

Evaluating Your Handling of the Communication Situation

As we have demonstrated throughout this text, your communication situation shapes the way that you write—even the number of revisions that are necessary. It should come as no surprise, therefore, that your first concern when revising should be evaluating whether you have accounted for the needs of your purpose and audience and whether you have established an appropriate tone, voice, and persona. Consequently, all of the questions that you asked during prewriting are equally relevant when revising. We therefore strongly recommend that you reconsider the questions for analyzing your purpose, audience, and tone which we introduced in chapter 1. In addition, because new insights may have occurred to you when writing, you should ask the questions on the checklist to evaluate how your perception of your purpose, audience, and tone has evolved.

In evaluating your tone, remember that there is no law that says you must be a stuffy writer and speaker. To the contrary, the move

Checklist for Revising: The Communication Situation

Purpose analysis

1. As I look over the whole, the paragraphs, the sentences, and the words, can I see new meaning emerging?
2. Did I finish with the same purpose that I began with? What changes to my introduction need to be made to account for what I have actually done?

Audience analysis

1. How has my opinion about who my audience is changed as a result of writing? Have I included all of the information that the particular audience needs to understand a particular event or concept? Have I written anything that might offend the audience or seem patronizing to the audience?
2. Have I thoroughly accounted for what my readers need to know? What terms or concepts need clarification?
3. Have I needlessly complicated the issue? If I have reviewed precedents, will my readers understand how they apply to the facts?
4. What changes do I need to make to help my audience better understand the subject?

Tone analysis

1. Have I established the voice that I set out to present? Are there any sections in which I appear confused, pedantic, irritable, stuffy?
2. Now that I have thought more deeply about the subject, have my thoughts changed about the particular voice that I should try to establish?
3. Do I keep a consistent tone throughout the document?

ment in the practice of law is away from the image of lawyers as Charles Dickens described them in his novels more than one hundred years ago, and still believed by some of the general public.

Identifying Gaps in Content Development and Reasoning

Poor reasoning on the author's part makes us wonder whether he or she is lacking in reasoning skills or in the time to do a careful job. And nothing is more frustrating than to feel as if the author has omitted details important to our understanding of the document. As writers, therefore, we need to ask the critical questions on the checklist.

Checklist for Revising: Content

1. What conceptual gaps now appear in my reasoning? Do I provide enough information so that the reader will feel that I have properly supported my contention or do I need to provide additional information?
2. Are my examples and illustrations effective? Can I provide examples to help readers visualize conceptual problems? Have I used concepts that my readers will not understand?
3. If I have presented an argument, will my readers find my sources to be credible? Am I relying too heavily on secondary sources?
4. Have I omitted too many details? Have I used the necessary details that my readers will need to understand the document?

Evaluating the Overall Organization of Your Document

When analyzing the overall plan you have for organizing a document, remember that your readers are not necessarily interested in the step-by-step process that you underwent to reach your conclusions, nor do they necessarily want a comprehensive review of the law that applies to your situation. Instead, readers generally expect you to sift through all of the facts and pertinent laws, and then they want you to state succinctly your interpretation and conclusions. Most legal and professional readers want to be presented information in a *deductive* manner—that is, they want to be told what they're going to be told, why it is important, and—in the conclusion—what they have been told.

Because your control over the idea is stronger now that you have written a draft, you should take a moment to reevaluate your overall organizing scheme. If, after rereading the document and jotting down notes about major themes in the margins of it, you still doubt your organization, you may want to draw a cluster or pie diagram or an issue tree (see chapter 2). Or, if time permits, you may draw a formal outline of it so that you can ensure that all subpassages relate to a major point. Asking the questions on the checklist should also help you transcend your writer-centered perspective and adopt a more reader-centered perspective.

Evaluating the Organization of Your Paragraphs

When drafting documents, you don't want to interrupt the flow of your thoughts to check on whether you are placing them in logical order. Eventually, however, you will need to reconsider all of your paragraphs in light of the questions on the checklist on page 142.

Checklist for Revising: Overall Organization

Questions for Revising Expository Documents

1. What is the overall organizing principle of my document? Am I organizing by topic and priority, by chronological order, by cause and effect? Have I organized my material deductively or inductively? Am I working from a problem to a solution or from a cause to an effect? Will another arrangement of the material be more effective?
2. Have I provided the necessary forecasting and transitional sentences that readers will need to understand how the different ideas relate to each other?
3. When describing *what* something is, have I effectively ranked the issues in their order of importance?
4. When explaining *how* something occurred, have I divided the issue or process into major steps?
5. When explaining *why* something happened, have I thoroughly explored all of the possible causes and effects? Have I avoided making a *post hoc* fallacy?
6. What changes in the format of my document will make my prose more readable? Should I use fewer or more subheadings? Can I use bullets or subheadings or lists to emphasize key points?
7. Can I use a picture, a graph, or a table to visually represent my meaning?

Questions for Revising Persuasive Documents

1. Are my logical appeals rock solid? Do my supporting points follow an effective, logical progression? What additional evidence or reasoning can I provide to be more convincing?
2. Have I presented appropriate ethical and emotional appeals?
3. Am I addressing a triadic or dyadic communication situation? Should I format my text as a traditional persuasion or more diplomatically, as described in the analysis of techniques for soft negotiation in chapter 13?

Reading Your Work Aloud

In a surprisingly powerful way, reading your work aloud highlights problems with your voice, content development, and grammar. Because of this, many writers mumble to themselves while they compose, and many successful writers read a final draft aloud to ensure that it is as effective as possible. Try it. You'll be surprised by its usefulness.

Checklist for Revising: Paragraph Organization

1. Should whole paragraphs be shifted in their order in the text?
2. Should the existing paragraphs be cut into smaller segments or merged into longer ones?
3. Should a later paragraph be combined with an earlier one?
4. Will readers understand the logical connections between paragraphs? Do any additional sentences need to be added to clarify the logical relationship between ideas?
5. Will reordering any sentences clarify the logic?

Soliciting Critiques from Colleagues

Unfortunately, many of us had few opportunities to work with other students on writing projects when we attended school. As a result, we are unprepared for coauthoring or editing other people's manuscripts. When colleagues ask you to critique their work, you may feel as if you're on soft ground. How specific, how honest, how thorough should we be? These sorts of questions can render us mute. In turn, if you believe in the myth of the isolated writer in the garret, then you put yourself under unrealistic pressure to draft a perfect document without the aid of your colleagues.

Because criticism is so important to creating exemplary documents, however, you should perceive criticism as an inevitable and positive part of making meaning. Experienced writers understand that criticism of a document is just that: criticism of the manuscript. A good critical reader is not impugning your character or your abilities as a writer or your potential as a writer. Instead, he or she is criticizing a manuscript, one particular event. When someone returns your work and says that your ideas need to be refined, you should not assume that you are a shallow thinker or that you cannot write. Instead, you must remember that most authors work their ideas through multiple drafts. Even though accepting criticism is difficult, we must view criticism as a form of help from our professional colleagues.

Of course, because different readers tend to look for different things in a text, you cannot always trust their advice. You need to remember that subjective factors can cloud a reader's evaluation. At the same time, you should try not to be overly discouraged or defensive about a reader's constructive response to your work.

These suggestions should help you profit most from the critiquing process.

1. Be careful about whom you ask to critique your work. Some of your colleagues will dislike anything that they didn't write themselves. Our experience working with lawyers and other professionals suggests that overly critical people tend to be blocked writers, so we suggest that you avoid them.
2. When you ask someone to critique your work, let him or her know the kind of feedback that you want. Give him or her a sense of how complete you believe your document is. Ask him or her to pay attention to particular issues, problems, and questions. For example, let him or her know if you are uncomfortable with your voice or purpose. Telling your colleagues that you are open for criticism—if it's true—helps break the ice.
3. Do not argue with your critics or expect them to revise your documents. Instead, consider your critics' ideas as a whole and then sift through their suggestions and revise accordingly. Be sure, however, to always follow your instinct: remember, even reasonable people tend to disagree.
4. When criticizing a colleague's documents, remember that authorship is ownership. Your proper role is consultant, not coauthor. When the purpose of the writer's work is unclear, do not necessarily assume that you know exactly what the writer hopes to do. It's much more helpful in the long run to express your confusion rather than make assumptions about what you think the writer is doing or hopes to do.
5. Try to limit the number of global, general comments such as, "I think the document is good." Although somewhat helpful, general responses are usually too vague to help your peers improve their work. Whenever possible, critique particular excerpts of your colleague's text. Give specific examples of what you mean from the text when you are critiquing; ask your colleagues to do the same.
6. Rank order your commentaries so that your colleagues know what you think needs most work. When offering your criticisms, couch them in an "I" message. Instead of saying, "This paragraph is weak," say, "I found this paragraph to be weak because it seemed to wander."

Checklist for Revising: Overall Process

1. Have you adopted an aggressive, fault-finding attitude? Have you considered whether you need to make major changes in organization?
2. Have you allowed time before the revision process so that you will be more likely to approach your document as your reader would?
3. How well have you handled the communication situation: purpose, audience, and tone? Have you changed your mind on the nature of any of these? Is the way you approached purpose, audience, and tone consistent throughout your document? (See the *Checklist for Revising: The Communication Situation* on page 139.)
4. Are there gaps in content or reasoning? Are your concepts well illustrated by examples? (See the *Checklist for Revising: Content* on page 140.)
5. Does the overall organization of your document work well? Will the reader be able to follow the sequence of ideas? (See the *Checklist for Revising: Overall Organization* on page 141.)
6. Are your paragraphs in a logical order and of appropriate length? (See the *Checklist for Revising: Paragraph Organization* on page 142.)
7. Have you read your document aloud to help you improve your voice and the flow of the sentences?
8. Have you asked colleagues to critique your document and make suggestions for improvement?

CHAPTER 16

Strategies for Improving Readability and Style

I know you lawyers can, with ease,
Twist words and meaning as you please;
That language, by your skill made pliant,
Will bend to favor every client;
That 'tis the fee directs the sense,
To make out either side's pretense,
When you peruse the clearest case,
You see it with a double face,
For scepticism is your profession;
You hold there's doubt in all expression.

—John Gay, *Fables*

Now that you have substantively revised your document by addressing the critical questions discussed in chapter 15, you probably feel good about it. Perhaps you shared a "working draft" with your colleagues and they complimented you on its effective, thorough treatment of the matter. The idea of continuing work on this document may seem pointless, even counterproductive.

Why continue reviewing the document? First, your readers make judgments about your professional abilities based on how well you write. You need to make your writing as smooth-sounding and clear as possible. You therefore cannot rest on compliments from in-house critics. After all, no one—not even the most diligent senior partner—has enough time to be as critical of your work as you can be (or need to be). Second, the observation that "Anything that can be misunderstood will be" is particularly accurate for legal writing. As you read over the document, you may notice ambiguous passages and sentences that may be interpreted in several ways. We, therefore, recommend that you continue playing *the doubting game.* With practice, you will find that the final edit often makes the difference between excellence and mediocrity.

This chapter introduces strategies that you can use to improve the readability of your prose. Our present focus becomes narrower than that presented in the previous chapter: here we limit our attention to *individual sentences* and *words.* Once you have used these strategies to copyedit your document along with the strategies for making substantive revisions that were analyzed in chapter 15, we are sure that your readers will judge your documents to be precise, vigorous, and economical.

Before discussing copyediting strategies, however, we feel impelled to remind you that these editorial concerns should be addressed *after* you have written a solid draft of your document. Considering these guidelines while writing can lead to writer's block and poor time management. Because these strategies are easier to conduct than those illustrated in chapter 15, you may need to fight the urge to copyedit rough drafts.

Reviewing for Sentence Length and Clear Sentence Patterns

A basic way to improve the readability of your document is to analyze the length of your sentences and the placement of subjects.

SENTENCE LENGTH

One of the most common problems with legal language is excessive sentence length. As you no doubt know from your practice, some lawyers love long, windy sentences. They enjoy snuggling citations between subjects and verbs. As illustrated by the following passage, a needlessly long sentence can make even simple ideas appear difficult.

> On or before March 1, 1976, plaintiff leased to defendants, Susan Wilson, also known as Susie Evans, and her husband, Robert Carlton, also known as Bill Henderson, the premises, consisting of the upstairs apartment and corral located at 1644 Lunar Road, West Central Texas, who, in consideration therefore, agreed to pay plaintiff the sum of $185.00 per month rent for the upstairs apartment and $12.50 per month for the corral payable monthly in advance, to commit no waste, and to maintain the premises.

Contrary to what you may have heard, however, long sentences are not necessarily ineffective or wordy. It is true that your average sentence length should be about 10 to 15 words for readers with a high-school education, about 15 to 20 words for readers with college education, and about 20 to 25 words for readers with advanced degrees. However, a memo with mostly short sentences can be just as ineffective as a memo with an average of 35 words per sentence, so you cannot view sentence length as the ultimate criterion by which to judge style. A string of short sentences conveys a grade-school style, and it requires readers to make logical connections between ideas on their own. Even a 35-word sentence may be perceived as highly readable by high-school-educated readers if it is effectively and elegantly shaped.

PLACE THE SUBJECT IN THE BEGINNING OF THE SENTENCE

To develop a successful style, you can vary the way you shape sentences. In addition to considering the average sentence length for a document, evaluate the demands that different sentence patterns make on your readers. As a general rule, you can improve the readability of your prose by limiting the number of words that come between the beginning of the sentence and its subject. One problem with long introductory phrases and clauses is that they strain the reader's short-term memory. Notice, for example, how you need to juggle all of the following conditions in your short-term memory when you read the following sentence:

> If the letter is not received before 6/14, or if the recipient has before that date sent a letter of rejection, or if, moreover, the recipient has not met all of the other terms of the offer, then, in that event, the contract is null and void.

Fortunately, most sentences with long introductory clauses such as this one can be easily repaired; all you need to do is move the concluding words—that is, the independent clause—to the beginning of the sentence, as in the following revision:

> The contract will go into effect if we receive a letter of acceptance by 6/14 and if the recipient has met all of the other terms of the offer.

Your legal training has made you more skilled than the average reader at holding groups of words in your short-term memory. After all, much legal writing contains long introductory phrases and clauses. However, when revising your documents for nonlawyers, you should realize that cognitive psychologists have determined that most people can hold only seven (plus or minus two) units of information in their short-term memory at a time. As a result, you need to realize that your reader's comprehension will diminish with each additional word or clause that you place before the subject of the sentence.

When copyediting your sentences, you should not attempt to eliminate all of the introductory words, phrases, and clauses. Instead, a more realistic goal would be to reduce their frequency to about 50 percent of the time. A few introductory clauses can help you establish a forceful rhythm, and your documents would put your readers to sleep if all of the sentences were shaped in the same way. Also, a transitional word or phrase can aid readability. *Therefore, however, on the other hand, as a result*—these sorts of words typically highlight how different ideas relate to each other. If used selectively and logically, these words and phrases actually help readers connect different ideas.

AVOID EXCESSIVE EMBEDDING BETWEEN THE SUBJECT AND THE VERB

Because they are often juggling numerous legal principles, lawyers are particularly fond of interrupting the flow of a sentence by embedding an appositive, participial phrase, or relative clause between the subject and the verb. (As you may recall from school, an appositive is a word or phrase that renames or redefines a noun or pronoun; a participle is a verb form that functions as an adjective, and a relative clause, which usually begins with *that, who* or *which,* is a dependent clause that offers additional information about a noun.)

As English speakers, we need to link a subject of a sentence to its verb to understand any statement. As a result, we must hold in our short-term memory all of the defining and modifying words that come between the subject and verb. As illustrated by the following passage, it is not until we reach the verb that we reach closure and fully understand what we are supposed to do with the subject:

> **Example:** The decision of Otis Clark, the plaintiff who is suing for breach of promise, having been informed of the offer that the defendant and his representatives have proposed as a settlement in light of the most recent developments, is now being awaited.

Just as it is impractical to eliminate all introductory causes from your documents, you should not attempt to eliminate all embedded appositives and modifiers. Embedding appositives or modifiers between subjects and verbs can enliven what is traditionally considered the least emphatic part of a sentence: that is, the middle part. Notice, for example, how the appositive in the following example, *the senior partner on the case,* emphasizes Fleming's position as an authority figure:

> **Example:** Jack Fleming, the senior partner on the case, wants your head!

Because this sentence pattern strains a reader's short-term memory, however, you should probably use it no more than about 5 to 10 percent of the time.

Using Active Rather Than Passive Voice and Avoiding *Be* Verbs

Most passive sentences are wordy, dull, and difficult to understand. Nine times out of ten, you should transform passive sentences into active ones. Surprisingly, however, the use of the passive voice is endemic in legal discourse. Sentences with *be* verbs tend to be inert.

PASSIVE v. ACTIVE VOICE

Why does the passive voice suck the energy from sentences? Essentially, a verb is *passive* when its subject is acted upon by an outside agent rather than doing the action. A passive verb is preceded by some form of the verb *to be (am, is, was, were, being, been)*, and the outside agent is often preceded by the preposition *by*. Notice in the following example how the transformation of the passive into the active enlivens the message:

> **Passive:** The plaintiff *was clubbed* repeatedly on the head by the defendant.
> **Active:** The defendant repeatedly clubbed the plaintiff on the head.

Notice, for example, how the message in the passage below gains vigor by being rewritten in the active voice:

> **Passive Voice:** This action was commenced by the filing of a complaint in the District Court of Hillsborough County on December 18, 1973. (R3). It is alleged in the complaint that the defendant Payson City Hospital is a separate entity and wholly owned proprietorship of Payson city and operated for profit. (R. 3-4, 8, 15.) It is further alleged that plaintiff Coralee Greenhalgh entered defendant hospital for childbirth on January 14, 1970, and that her infant son, plaintiff Patrick Greenhalgh, was born at the hospital on the same date (R. 4, 8, 11, 15.); and that defendant hospital was negligent in incorrectly blood-typing the two plaintiffs, and that by reason thereof, and by reason of failure timely to discover this error, both plaintiffs sustained serious personal injuries. (R. 9, 10, 16.) It is further alleged that . . .

> **Active Voice:** The plaintiffs, Coralee and Patrick Greenhalgh, commenced this action by filing a complaint in the District Court of Hillsborough County on December 18, 1973. (R. 3) against Payson City Hospital. The plaintiff contends that Payson City Hospital is a separate entity and wholly owned proprietorship of Payson City and is operated for profit. (R. 3-4, 8, 15.) The plaintiffs allege that Coralee Greenhalgh entered Payson City

Hospital for childbirth on January 14, 1970, and that her infant son, plaintiff Patrick Greenhalgh, was born at the hospital on the same date (R. 4, 8, 11, 15.). The complaint alleges that defendant hospital was negligent in incorrectly blood-typing the two plaintiffs, which caused the plaintiffs serious personal injuries. (R. 9, 10, 16.) The complaint further alleges that . . .

While the passive voice strangles the life from most legal discourse, we should add that it has some legitimate uses. For example, you may want to use the passive voice when you do not know who is responsible for an action, when the actual person who performed the action has no relevance, or when you wish to hide this information from readers. Thus, a spokesperson for a chemical company would be more likely to say, "Toxic chemicals have been found on the vacant property," rather than "John Q. Public, Chief Environmental Scientist for X Company, found toxic chemicals on the vacant property."

ELIMINATE *BE* VERBS

In our daily speech and rough drafts, we tend to rely heavily on the various forms of the verb *be.* Beyond being boring because of its overuse, the verb *to be* is unlike any other verb because it is inert—that is, it does not show any action. For example, in the sentence "The defendant is a six-foot-tall, 200-pound male Caucasian," the verb *is* merely connects the subject with what grammarians call the *subject complement.* We could just as easily write "A six-foot, 200-pound male Caucasian is the defendant" without changing the meaning. In a sense, a linking verb works like the equal sign in mathematical equations: it links a subject to a subject complement without expressing any action.

A document with a surfeit of *be* verbs can often be improved by taking the action out of the nouns and putting it into the verbs.

Example: The decision of the client was not to accept the offer.
Revision: The client declined the offer.

It would be nearly impossible to draft documents without some linking verbs. Yet because the vigor of your sentences diminishes with each is and are that you use, you should try to limit their frequency to about 25 percent of your sentences.

Finally, please note that the *progressive form* of a verb—which involves the use of the verb *be* as an auxiliary verb with a participle—is not a form of the verb *be* to be avoided. The progressive illustrates action progressing over time and should be used wherever you need to express this meaning:

The defendant *is hitting* (*was hitting* or *had been hitting*) the plaintiff for good reason.

AVOID *IT IS* AND *THERE IS/ARE* CONSTRUCTIONS

As suggested by the discussion of *be* verbs, *it is* and *there is/are* constructions lead to sluggish, weak sentences, so you should ruthlessly eliminate them from your documents. Of course, avoiding all *it is* and *there is/are* constructions is not feasible: they sometimes allow you to be more succinct than by placing the true subject at the beginning of the sentence, and they sometimes help you lead into a topic. As a general rule, however, you should treat *it is* and *there is/are* constructions as seeds of a deadly virus. Sentences such as "It is clearly a fact that the defendant struck the plaintiff repeatedly in the head with a chair" can invariably be improved by eliminating the weak beginning.

Using Precise, Economical, Jargon-free Language

Your writing gains vigor and precision when you avoid needless abstractions and redundancies.

AVOID VAGUE, ABSTRACT LANGUAGE

Avoiding vague language does not mean that you need to go into monotonous detail about facts or concepts that your readers are likely to know. What this does mean is that you should critically evaluate every word that you use, asking "Will my reader understand me here?"

Note how the following opening passage to an in-house memo on lawyers' salaries lacks the specifics you need to understand the message:

> **Specific Performance Criteria.** While establishing a system of lawyers' compensation is never easy, the Committee cannot rest upon generalizations in establishing specific salary levels. Those concepts are generic in nature and intentionally undefined. Standing alone, they are subject to wide and vastly different interpretations.
>
> On the other hand, slide rule–type formulas, while easy in application and yielding finite and very specific results, are often blind to many of the relevant factors which should be taken into account in setting compensation levels that are in the best interests of both the individual lawyer and the Firm. As such, neat formulas, which are unadjusted or unweighted for various elements that are not given to mathematical precision, are almost always dangerous. Their use is, of course, appealing for arithmetic cuts across areas of subjectivity and debate, and produces an automatic result. Moreover, formula compensation proposals that do not account for all the rel-

> evant elements may be used by a member of the Firm to argue a selfish position, causing ill will and harsh feelings. It is not too much to add that this Firm has the reverse psyche and has been founded in an atmosphere of good will, fair dealing, and trustworthiness.

As you can well imagine, attorneys interested in their salaries would be curious about what "generic and intentionally undefined" concepts the author refers to in the opening paragraph. What are the "relevant factors" that slide-rule formulas neglect to account for? If these factors could be accounted for, would the author still consider slide-rule formulas to be dangerous? When addressing such an emotionally charged subject, you need to be particularly careful to define your terms as they are introduced. You add punch to your sentences by replacing abstract words with details and specifics. Wherever possible, you should try to use *concrete* words—words that represent actual physical things like "chair" and "house"—and *sensory* words—words that appeal to people's five senses.

AVOID REDUNDANT LANGUAGE

In your search for precision, you should also delete unnecessary repetitions. Of course, you are understandably anxious to report everything necessary to help you explain a case or argue persuasively. Yet by deleting redundant adjectives, repeated phrases, and synonyms, your writing will gain in clarity and persuasive appeal. Notice how the following revision, for example, omits the sluggish, lazy tone of the original:

> **Example:** At that time, Plaintiff, suffering from severe mental illness, was involuntarily committed to a psychiatric facility in Boston where she was diagnosed as being mentally ill and was thus mentally impaired.
>
> **Revision:** In December 1989, the plaintiff was involuntarily committed to a psychiatric facility in Boston where she was diagnosed with mental illness.

To determine the most appropriate word choice for a document, you must consider your audience and purpose. For example, you may know a few readers who believe legal writing must be obscure, vague, and jargon-ridden. After all, some members of the profession take great joy in sounding as sophisticated as possible. With the sense that their thoughts are being embossed on golden tablets, some writers believe that they should use sophisticated-sounding words. After writing drafts with solid, common words, these writers use the thesaurus feature on their word processing program or reach for a bound thesaurus and unnecessarily change direct language into more formal language or legal jargon.

Long or Formal Word	**Use Instead**
abrogate	give up
apprise	inform
contingent upon	dependent on
endeavor	try
initiate	begin
promulgate	publish
utilize	use

It is also true that lawyers distinguish themselves by employing awkward syntactical structures and by saturating memoranda and briefs with statutory language, obscure Latin phrases, and strings of synonymous words. Ever mindful of precedent and eager to avoid unnecessary litigation, lawyers have traditionally been reluctant to change legal language so that it reflects change in everyday English usage. For example, when English courts decided that court proceedings should be carried on in English rather than Latin or French, lawyers translated many of the Latin and French words and then added them to the English words instead of just using the most accurate English word. Because of this fear of leaving out information, many modern documents contain unnecessary synonymous words, such as *acknowledge and confess, in truth and in fact, authorize and empower, cease and desist.* The continued presence of these redundant synonyms in legal discourse highlights the resistance that some members of the legal community have for plain language.

You, however, should delete any strings of words that carry obvious redundant messages, such as *true and accurate, first and foremost, any and all, true facts, future plans, consensus of opinion.* Most of the political and communication situations that you address as a legal writer will require you to communicate as succinctly and persuasively as possible. Few readers are impressed by the use of Latin or French words that are not terms of art when more understandable English words can be used that are just as precise. *In esse* (in being), *in invitum* (without consent), *nil* (nothing), *alien* (to transfer property), *save* (except)—these sorts of words add static rather than precision to legal documents.

As we illustrated throughout Part I, you need to evaluate your communication situation to determine what information should be provided in any given document. By analyzing your audience and purpose, you will be able to determine what references are necessary to communicate your point. Because you are usually more informed about the elements of the law than your audience, you need to remember to educate your readers about the precedents that you raise. Can you see how, for example, a less informed audience would feel when reading the following case references?

> Courts have tightened up the standards for scienter for secondary (aiding and abetting) violators. E.g. *Woods v. Barnett Bank*, 765 F. 2d 1004, 1010 (11th Cir. 1985) ("severe recklessness" instead of "mundane recklessness"); see also Louis Loss, *Fundamentals of Securities Regulations* 1185 (1983) (suggesting that actual knowledge is required for secondary liability); *Hakama v. E.F. Hutton & Co., Inc.*, 566 F. Supp. 636 *C.D.1 1983) (courts have generally declined to impose liability absent knowledge of the violation).

This passage is clearly troubled by a lack of parallelism among the phrases inside the parentheses. (The first parenthetical element—*severe recklessness instead of mundane recklessness*—is not the grammatical equivalent of the following parenthetical elements, a participial phrase—*suggesting that actual knowledge is required for secondary liability*, and the third element, a sentence—*courts have generally declined to impose liability absent knowledge of the violation*). Yet the problems with this passage extend beyond any confusion caused by a grammatical *faux pas*. Because the information within the parentheses is so abbreviated, it leaves the reader wanting more, speculating "Is the author trying to put one over on me here?"

Maintaining a High Verb-to-Noun Ratio and Avoiding Strings of Nouns

One effective way to make your writing more direct and easier to read is to focus on your use of nouns: you should examine nominalizations (i.e., nouns formed from verbs) and long strings of nouns to see if more forceful or clearer constructions can be used in their place.

ESTABLISH A HIGH VERB-TO-NOUN RATIO

You can make your language more precise and vigorous by having a high verb-to-noun ratio. You should therefore review your documents to determine whether any nouns can be deleted or transformed into verbs.

You can easily change Latinate nouns—that is, nouns ending with *-ance, -ion, -tion, -ment,* and *-ure*—into verbs.

Ending	Noun	Verb
-ance	assistance	assist
-ion	decision	decide
-tion	reduction	reduce
-ment	movement	move
-ure	failure	fail

Here is a simple example showing how you can make your writing more direct by replacing a Latinate noun (*investigation*) with a verb:

> **Original:** A representative from the state welfare department conducted an investigation into the bus company's safety procedures.
>
> **Revision:** A representative from the state welfare department investigated the bus company's safety procedures.

Notice in this more complex example how changing the two occurrences of the noun *examination* into verbs adds clarity and conciseness to the rough draft.

> **Original:** Examination of the doctor's alleged misconduct was commenced by the Grand Jury. The present intention of the Grand Jury is to conduct a thorough examination of the doctor's medical records.
>
> **Revision:** The Grand Jury plans to examine the doctor's alleged misconduct by thoroughly studying the doctor's medical records.

AVOID STRINGS OF NOUNS

Although some conservative grammarians assert that nouns should not be used as modifiers, this construction is common in English: Who would want to replace *college education* with *collegial education, science fiction* with *scientific fiction*, or *law student* with *legal student?* As usual, moderation is the key. What you should try to avoid is long strings of nouns modifying a noun, as in this example:

> the trial brief fact section contents
> **Instead:** the contents of the fact section in a trial brief

This is one case where the addition of words makes the phrase clearer: the use of the prepositions in the revision shows how the various words modifying the noun *contents* are to be grouped. Otherwise, there can be ambiguity in how to interpret the relationship among the nouns in the string.

Some noun strings, however, are part of technical language and are in common use. With many of these, you can use hyphens to help show the relationship among the nouns: *sleep-disorders medicine.* In cases where the first noun modifies the final two, hyphens are not used: *city corporation counsel, government labor arbitrator.*

Using the First Person Where Appropriate

"Do not use the first person" is perhaps the most pernicious recommendation that English teachers make. After all, how can we think without using our experience? Why must we drive a stake through our cerebral cortex before writing?

Now it is certainly true that use of the first person can be obtrusive. In many situations, use of the third person and the passive voice is required by convention. When writing a brief, for instance, your focus is more on the law, so personal comments would be superfluous and impertinent. In contrast, just as you would wear running gear rather than a three-piece business suit to run in a road race, you would not want to use the third person or passive voice when writing an informal memo to a member of your firm. If you have not written much in the first person or if you tend to be a shy person, you may at first feel exposed when using the first person, yet with time it will become natural. In fact, because of its seminal role in invention, some writing experts suggest writing all drafts in the first person—even those that will need to be transformed into the third person or passive voice.

Transforming Negatives into Affirmatives

When you read the following sentence, do you find yourself backtracking, saying "Huh?":

> Experts do not disagree in their disapproval for authors who do not pay attention to the rule not to use negatives.

As a skilled lawyer, you surely are a master of the double negative. As a writer who wants to avoid unnecessary misunderstandings, however, you must avoid negative phrases. Your language will invariably be briefer and more understandable if you write in the affirmative.

Editing Strings of Prepositional Phrases

Understandably, you are getting sick and tired of looking at your manuscript at this point. You have examined the structure of your sentences and evaluated their impact on your reader's short-term memory, ensured that you have substituted affirmative phrases for negative ones, and transformed nouns into verbs and maintained a high verb-to-noun ratio. Yet before you consider yourself through with copyediting your document, you should take a hard look at the number of prepositional phrases you have used.

When used in moderation, prepositions are invaluable. Few sentences can be written without them. Essentially, prepositions work as connecting words: they link the object of the preposition to the preposition, and they link the object of the preposition to a word that appears earlier in the sentence. Readers must gather together the chunks of meaning the prepositional phrases provide in order to understand the sentence. When used excessively, as demonstrated by the following example, prepositional phrases create a choppy, list-like style:

> Dr. Harvey Wong testified that he was familiar *with* medical literature published *before* 1967 indicating the hazards *of* detergent contamination, that he was aware *of* the use *of* detergents *by* the City Hospital *in* the cleansing *of* its instruments and that he considered this *in* accordance *with* the standard *of* care *of* this community *at* that time, particularly *in* view *of* the excellent record *of* no untoward incidents *over* a long period *of* time.

By changing strings of prepositional phrases into other constructions *(that he was aware of the use of detergents by the City Hospital in the cleansing of its instruments)* and by omitting vague phrases that seem unnecessary (such as *over a long period of time*), we can improve clarity and write a sentence that is fourteen words shorter:

> Dr. Harvey Wong testified that he was familiar *with* medical literature published *since* 1967 that identified hazards *with* detergent contamination, that he knew City Hospital used these detergents to cleanse its instruments, and that he considered this usage acceptable because the detergent had an excellent record *of* no untoward incidents and met the standards *of* care established *by* this community.

Review of Copyediting for Readability

The following checklist summarizes basic points to help you improve the flow and clarity of your sentences and to help you improve your word choice.

Checklist for Copyediting Sentences

1. Have you reviewed your sentence length and sentence patterns? Do you generally have sentences of 20 to 25 words for professional audiences and less than 20 for other audiences?
2. Have you placed the subject in the beginning of many sentences?
3. Have you avoided excessive embedding between the subject and the verb?
4. Have you used active instead of passive verbs?
5. Have you avoided inert *be* verbs?
6. Have you avoided using *it is* and *there is/are?*
7. Have you edited for both vague and redundant language?
8. Have you reviewed your sentences, changing nouns to verbs, in order to have a high verb-to-noun ratio?
9. Have you used the first person where appropriate in informal documents?
10. Have you transformed negatives into affirmatives?
11. Have you revised strings of prepositional phrases?
12. Have you avoided unnecessary jargon and inflated prose?

CHAPTER 17

Strategies for Copyediting Documents

Now that you have used the strategies illustrated in chapters 15 and 16 for making substantive revisions, you are probably sick and tired of looking at the manuscript. In fact, a cloudy haze may obscure your vision and an overpowering feeling of exhaustion may overcome you when it comes time to do a final copyedit of the document. After all, you say to yourself, I have been through it a dozen times, so there cannot be any errors!

But there are errors. Lots of them. This is the nature of the beast. Of course, you can blame the typist for introducing errors when entering the last revisions. (On a political level, though, you should probably blame the word processing program. After all, it will not walk out on you.)

Doing a final copyedit means reviewing your document to ensure that spelling, grammar, punctuation, and capitalization are correct. This chapter offers a concise review of the rules and myths of punctuation. We discuss the various ways to punctuate different sentence patterns, and we analyze the likely effect of these syntactical forms on your reader's comprehension.

Using Commas Correctly

Commas are like pawns in chess: they seem relatively insignificant and unobtrusive, yet they are actually very important. If properly placed, the lowly pawn can checkmate the king or, once it has reached the end of the board, become a more powerful piece. Commas play an extremely important role in ensuring that your documents are understandable. For example, if you are representing a wealthy client who desperately wants to purchase some land, you need to know the difference between, "No price too high" and "No, price too high" when settling on a purchase price. As we explore below, the failure to produce a comma in the correct spot can cause considerable misreading (and subsequent embarrassment). Beyond a few special circumstances, there are four basic ways to use commas correctly.

USE COMMAS TO SEPARATE ITEMS IN A SERIES

As demonstrated by the following examples, a series is composed of three or more *parallel* elements, and the series can appear in the beginning, middle, or end of a sentence:

> Stretching, warming-up, and cooling-down are important to a good exercise program.

> All of the necessary qualities of a good secretary—typing, shorthand, and patience—she had in abundance.

> The three qualities of a good introduction are context, purpose, and organization.

Although many standard textbooks and stylebooks recommend that a comma should be placed before the last element in a series, there is variation in this usage. The trend in the popular press is *not* to include the comma if the elements in the series are brief. However, Follett and Cook, two well-known stylists, have persuasively argued that conjunctions *connect* and commas *separate,* so it is incorrect in their opinion to judge the comma as redundant punctuation after a conjunction such as *and.* In addition, these stylists note that uninformed readers may perceive the last two elements in the series to be a compound. For example, placement of the comma before *and* in the following sentence would make it clear that it is not authorities who are to be avoided:

> The argument for using a comma before the last element in a series depends on convention, avoidance of ambiguity and authorities.

As a result, we recommend that you use a comma before the conjunction *(and, but, or)* in series of three or more items for clarity and ease of reading.

Occasionally, as dictated by your ear and the rhythm you hope to establish in your prose, you may want to insert a comma and forego the *and,* as in the following example:

> We have a government of the people, by the people, for the people.

When you want to slow down the rhythm of your sentence and emphasize a point, you can replace your commas with *and* or *or:*

> He does not like shrimp or crayfish or lobster or anything else that turns red when cooked.
>
> If the abuse of the wetlands continues, we will be without waterfowl and fish and wildlife.

When you must present a long list of parallel elements in your documents, you can avoid listing them by grouping them into logical parts and punctuating accordingly, as demonstrated by the following examples:

> Writing is painful and exhilarating, tedious and inspiring, chaotic and planned.
>
> Human activities such as coal and oil burning, population growth and increased food demands, clearing and burning forests have caused increases in the release of carbon dioxide and methane.

Finally, note that coequal, consecutive coordinate adjectives that modify the same noun should generally be separated with commas:

> Although he appears to have your best interests in mind, he truly is competitive, combative, cantankerous.

However, you should not separate two consecutive adjectives with commas if the first adjective is modifying the following adjective and noun, as illustrated below:

> **Not:** Short, introductory phrases are followed by commas.
> **Instead:** Short introductory phrases are followed by commas.

USE COMMAS TO SEPARATE TWO OR MORE INDEPENDENT CLAUSES JOINED BY A COORDINATING CONJUNCTION

In most instances, you should place a comma between two sentences that are joined with a coordinating conjunction—*and, but, or, for, nor, so, yet:*

> She was not sure if she had the necessary mathematical abilities to be an engineer, so she pursued a graduate degree in history.
>
> He was surrounded by some fifty people, yet he felt all alone.

You do not need to place a comma between two independent clauses if they are short and similar in meaning, provided that no misunderstanding will take place, as illustrated in the following examples:

> Some lawyers abuse the right to advertise their services and many other lawyers find this reprehensible. *(The absence of the comma in this sentence is acceptable, since it is not necessary to prevent misreading.)*

> There was a falling out between the parties, and the defendant would not give the plaintiff his complete share. *(Failure to place a comma after* parties *could cause the reader to think, on first reading, that* defendant *was part of a compound with* parties.)

USE COMMAS AFTER INTRODUCTORY CLAUSES AND PHRASES

To avoid confusion and to ensure ease of reading, place a comma after introductory clauses and phrases:

> Because of the high costs of conducting legal research, we need to raise our rates.

> As the shrimp boats trawl, sea grass can collect on the trap door, allowing shrimp to escape.

> According to the professor, rich women are more likely to have caesarean sections when giving birth than poor women.

In keeping with the modern trend toward using as little punctuation as possible, some stylists believe that it is not necessary for you to place a comma after introductory words *(thus, hence, first)* and short introductory phrases *(In 1982 he committed the same crime)*. However, in the conservative world of legal discourse, you are better off playing it safe than sorry: we recommend placing a comma after introductory phrases and clauses.

Included under this rule are conjunctive adverbs (for example, *therefore, however, otherwise*) and transitional phrases. When these types of words occur at the beginning of sentences, place a comma after them to separate them from the rest of the sentence:

> Nevertheless, we must push forward with our plans. In other words, you're fired. Hey, I'm just kidding.

Although logic would suggest that it makes sense to follow coordinating conjunctions with commas, convention does not call for this usage. Thus, it would be inappropriate to write "Yet, I think we should go ahead as planned." When a short phrase follows the conjunction at the beginning of a sentence, however, it is appropriate—although not absolutely necessary—to place a comma after the conjunction: "Yet, despite this, I think we should go ahead as planned."

USE COMMAS AROUND NONRESTRICTIVE PARENTHETICAL ELEMENTS

As mentioned in our earlier discussion of readability guidelines, you should limit the number of times that you interrupt the flow of a sentence by placing modifying words between the subject of a sentence and its verb. When you do introduce appositives, participial phrases, or adjective phrases or clauses between the subject and its verb or in other places in a sentence, you must determine whether the modifiers are *restrictive* or *nonrestrictive.* Commas are used with nonrestrictive modifiers; no commas are used with restrictive modifiers. Briefly, restrictive modifiers add information that is *essential* to the meaning of the sentence, whereas nonrestrictive modifiers add information that is *not essential* to understanding the gist of the sentence. To determine whether the modifier is restrictive or nonrestrictive, therefore, you need to ask whether taking it out changes the original meaning of the sentence.

> **Restrictive:** Lawyers who work for McGullity, Anderson and Swenson need to take a course in copyediting. *(In this case, the relative clause is essential to the meaning of the sentence. If you set off the clause with commas, then the meaning would change, suggesting that all lawyers need a course in copyediting.)*
>
> **Restrictive:** The lawyer who has worked on this case for three years thinks that we have no chance of winning. *(In this case the relative clause is essential to the meaning of the sentence. It is necessary to identify the particular lawyer. In other words, the sentence "The lawyer thinks that we have no chance of winning" would not state the author's original point.)*
>
> **Nonrestrictive:** The lawyers, who have an office downtown, think that we have no chance of winning. *(If the location of the lawyers' office is superfluous to the gist of the sentence and is not essential to identifying the lawyers who are being discussed, then the clause should be set off with commas.)*

At the end of your sentence, you need to be especially careful about where you place your commas. In particular, you need to question whether the modifying words are *restrictive* or *nonrestrictive.* For instance, if you received a memo from a senior partner that said, "You should argue the case, as I suggested," then you could assume that you were directed to argue the case in any way you deem appropriate. However, if the senior partner omitted the comma, then you would be receiving an entirely different message: conduct the case exactly as prescribed by the senior partner.

Below are some additional sentences to give you a sense of how to determine whether your modifying words are restrictive or nonrestrictive:

> **Nonrestrictive:** Reports indicate that a Turtle Excluder Device (TED) costs from $85 to $400 each, depending on the model.

> **Restrictive:** Writers can change readers' outlooks on issues provided that they offer sufficient evidence. *(In this case, a comma after* issues *could suggest that writers have numerous ways to change readers' opinions and that one of these methods is providing sufficient evidence. In contrast, the lack of a comma means that providing evidence is the one criterion writers need to follow.)*

Using Colons as a Stylistic Device

The colon provides a dramatic and somewhat underused way to bring a little spark to your writing. Beyond its use in the salutation in normal business correspondence *(Dear Sir or Madam:)*, you can use the colon before quotations, formal statements, explanations. The colon enables you to highlight a semantic relationship—that is, a movement from a general statement to a specific clarification.

As Jerold S. Auerbach demonstrates in the following example, the colon provides a dramatic way to tease the reader's curiosity:

> As a modern ordeal by torture, litigation excels: it is exorbitantly expensive, agonizingly slow, and exquisitely designed to avoid any resemblance to fairness or justice.

You can also use the colon before a phrase:

> An intelligent law clerk knows how to play at a firm-sponsored tennis tournament: look good losing the point.

Although usage does differ, most stylists agree that you should not capitalize the first letter after the colon unless the colon is introducing a quotation, as in the example below:

> You'll be surprised by what his former employees wrote in the character report: "His attitude toward his new associates was rude and pretentious."

Please note that the colon must always follow an independent clause. You should *never* place a colon between a verb and its direct object:

> **Incorrect Usage:** Our choices are: rescind our offer; go ahead with our plans; try to renegotiate the deal.

This sentence can easily be revised: "We have three choices: a, b, c" or

"Our choices are the following: a, b, c." Because the colon works as the equivalent to *for example* or *such as,* it would be redundant and incorrect to write "We have a number of options, such as: a, b, c."

Using Dashes and Parentheses Effectively

Some stylists view the dash with great suspicion—the sort of suspicion that would be offered to a guy in the 1990s who wears a plaid leisure suit to work. Some people erroneously believe that the dash is only acceptable in informal discourse. However, as we demonstrate below, the dash can provide you with subtle ways to repeat modifiers and dramatic ways to emphasize your point.

USE THE DASH AFTER A SERIES OR LIST OF APPOSITIVES

When you introduce a long series or list of appositives before the subject, you are placing high demands on the reader's short-term memory. We therefore recommend that you use this pattern rarely and only for emphasis. This pattern is, however, particularly appropriate when you are bringing together in one place the major threads of your argument. You can place a *summary word* after the dash and preferably before the subject of the sentence, as indicated by the following examples. The most common summary words that writers use are *all, those, this, each, what, none, such, these.*

> Intrigue, lust, hate, greed—*these* are the raw emotions we must explore.
>
> Lying, stealing, cheating, committing adultery—*which* is the greatest sin?
>
> To struggle with meaning, to edit, to combine listlike sentences—*these* activities are well known to the struggling writer.
>
> Wining and dining his friends, stroking people's egos, maintaining a good appearance, and spending money—*these* were all part of his scheme to gain influence.

USE THE DASH WHEN YOU WISH TO EMPHASIZE A PARENTHETICAL ELEMENT

Earlier we mentioned that commas are sufficient punctuation to set off parenthetical elements. In this instance, you also can use a dash if you want to make the insertion more noticeable:

> The building next to ours—the one with the all cedar exterior—was engulfed in flames.

When you want to whisper rather than shout, you can place the modifiers inside parentheses:

> The secret I have to tell you (the one I've been hinting about) will surprise you.

USE A DASH TO EMBED A SERIES OR LIST OF APPOSITIVES

While a single appositive or modifier can easily be set off from the rest of the sentence in commas, you should use dashes when a series of appositives or modifiers is introduced. After all, how else could the reader know when the series was over and when the flow of the sentence was beginning again?

> The essential qualities of an effective writer—discipline, effort, inspiration—he learned by regular writing.

> With the help of her assistant—a high-speed personal computer—she produced a delightful letter.

USE A DASH TO SET OFF AN EMPHATIC REPETITION

You can emphasize an important point by placing a dash or comma at the end of the sentence and then repeating a key word or phrase:

> Hal is a computer, the ultimate computer.

> Mrs. Leavitt is a gambler, a compulsive gambler.

> He was disturbed by the warning—the warning that was ignored by all the others.

> All rapists should be severely punished—punished in a way they will never forget.

Using Semicolons Appropriately

The semicolon offers a stronger form of punctuation than the comma or dash. Unlike commas or dashes, you can correctly use the semicolon to separate sentences. While readers tend to pause for a half second when coming to a comma, they pause for a three-quarter second when coming to a semicolon. As we show below, you have two major ways to use the semicolon correctly.

USE THE SEMICOLON TO JOIN TWO SENTENCES

You can show that ideas are closely related to each other by using a semicolon rather than a period to join two sentences:

> The secretary's fingers burned across the typewriter; the financial statements would be picked up by the client in one hour.

> The question, though, is not economics; it is professional objectivity.
>
> Breast cancer used to be the biggest killer of women; now it's lung cancer.

USE THE SEMICOLON TO PUNCTUATE A SERIES THAT HAS COMMAS

As we discussed earlier, a simple series can be punctuated with commas. A sentence such as "We are fortunate to have a government of the people, by the people, or for the people" does not require semicolons. However, when one of the elements of the series requires commas to ensure clarity, then semicolons must be used to separate the remaining elements:

> A perfect vacation *would be* long, relaxing, and cheap; *would include* personable, sweet, flexible people; and *would make* everything else seem trivial.
>
> To make a fishing trip successful, you *must have* the right bait—live pinfish, live shrimp, or a big dead mullet; must be in a good spot—a bridge or jetty; and *must have* plenty of luck.
>
> A good proofreader *must* have good grammar, punctuation, and spelling skills; *must* like to read; and *must* have patience.

We should note, however, that you are wise to avoid using unnecessary semicolons. Experienced writers and readers would prefer the second sentence because it avoids *self-conscious* punctuation.

> He was dressed in white pants; a white, Mexican wedding shirt; and sandals.
>
> **Preferred:** He was dressed in a white, Mexican wedding shirt, white pants, and sandals.

Final Copyediting Strategies

The checklist on page 169 summarizes some of the key points you should keep in mind as you do the final copyedit on your document, reviewing spelling, grammar, punctuation, and capitalization.

Frankly, at this stage of your document's development, you should farm it out to a copyeditor. It simply is not cost-effective for you or any other lawyer in your firm to spend more time on it. If your firm does not employ a copyeditor to do a final check of the documents, you should probably speak with the senior partners to arrange for hiring one. Meanwhile, if circumstances require that you do the final copyedit, we recommend the following strategies:

1. Consider each line of the text separately, using two sheets of paper to cover the rest of the text. To help focus on grammatical and mechanical errors, try reading your documents backwards—that is, from right to left and bottom to top. By beginning at the end of the document and considering each sentence separately, you can break the "semantic flow"—that is, the tendency to read for meaning rather than editorial correctness. You may have an easier time locating formatting errors by looking at the text upside down.
2. Do not try to copyedit a document all at once. Instead, alternate proofreading with other activities.
3. Change the location and time of day that you do your most important copyediting.
4. Look especially for errors in the opening paragraphs of documents and for errors in paragraphs that begin new sections. Skim through the document and check all of the headings and subheadings to ensure that they are spelled and formatted correctly. Look for errors in parallelism and in pronoun agreement. Check to see that no numbers were skipped or repeated if you have numbered points or headings.
5. Look for mistakes to cluster. When you find one error in paragraph seven, for example, you should carefully examine the surrounding sentences to see if you had a lapse of concentration when you wrote and revised that section.
6. Look for errors that you commonly make. For example, do you often use the plural antecedent for a singular pronoun—as in "The company should have been more careful about stating their [sic] hiring guidelines in print"?

You do reach a point at which your continued work on the manuscript is counterproductive. If you tend to be a perfectionist, you may need to work extra hard at letting go. Eventually your apprenticeship as a writer and legal thinker is better served by writing a new document. So you need to realize that every memo cannot be the Gettysburg Address. You cannot spend eternity working on each document. Prioritize each activity from most and least important and then work to gain perspective.

A Final Note on Viewing Writing as a Lifelong Apprenticeship

Now that you are familiar with prewriting, drafting, revising, and copyediting strategies, you possess all of the tools necessary to write well. Although your knowledge of the composing process cannot guarantee you immediate success, your understanding of how writers work should help you overcome writer's block and get a solid draft done in a reasonable amount of time.

Just as your understanding of the law deepens with time, so does your mastery of the writing process. Your thinking and your writing become a natural part of your life. Soon your best times will be before your word processor or dictating machine. Meanwhile, we wish you the best and hope that you will find, as we have, that writing can be a vital way to enrich your thinking and provide personal satisfaction.

Checklist for Final Copyediting

Spelling:

Have you checked all the words about which you are unsure of the spelling.

Grammar:

Have you reviewed the document for correct grammar, focusing on those points that give you particular difficulty? Some common points to look for are these:

1. Have you avoided run-on sentences? These are two sentences written as one, with only a comma or with no punctuation separating them.
2. Do all subjects and verbs agree in number? Have you checked that the subject of the sentence, not any following prepositional phrases, determines the number of the verb?
3. Do all pronouns have a clear antecedent so that you can tell to which word each pronoun is referring?
4. Are modifiers placed near the words they modify so that the relationship among phrases is clear?
5. Have you used *who/whom* correctly?

Punctuation:

Commas

1. Have you used commas to separate items in a series, placing one before the coordinating conjunction?
2. Have you used commas to separate two or more sentences joined by a coordinating conjunction?
3. Have you used commas after introductory clauses and phrases?
4. Have you used commas around nonrestrictive parenthetical elements?

Checklist for Final Copywriting (continued)

Colons

Have you used colons as a stylistic device to highlight a semantic relationship between sentences: a movement from general to specific?

Dashes and Parentheses

1. Have you used dashes as a stylistic device after a series of appositives?
2. Have you used dashes (instead of parentheses) when you want to highlight a parenthetical element?
3. Have you used dashes to embed a series of appositives?
4. Have you used dashes to set off emphatic repetition?

Semicolons

1. Have you used semicolons to join two sentences (when there is no coordinating conjunction between them)?
2. Have you used semicolons to punctuate a series that has commas?

Capitalization:

Have you used conventions for capitalization in your document and capitalized consistently throughout the document?

APPENDIXES:

Materials Relating to the Case Study

Appendix I

Exhibit A: Newspaper Article About the Ames Case

8-Year-Old Girl Run Over by School Van

TAMPA—An eight-year-old school girl was reported in stable condition today in Tampa Children's Hospital after being run over Tuesday by a school van.

The victim, Susan Ames, was rushed first to Northeast Tampa General Hospital after being struck and run over by a school van operated by Busarus. The girl reportedly darted in front of the van as it was about to pull away from the school where it had dropped her off moments before, according to police. The girl, deaf since birth, attends the Brinkman School for the Impaired.

The girl reportedly suffered multiple injuries to the head, legs, and neck. She was air-lifted by police Medi-Vac helicopter to Northeast General where she received emergency treatment. Later the same day she was transferred to Children's Hospital.

Patrol officers John Smith and Robert Brown conducted the investigation at the scene of the accident. Police said no citation was issued against the driver of the van.

Exhibit B: Police Report on the Ames Case

State of Florida
Police Report of Motor Vehicle Accident

Operator: James Wilson Driver's License #634-27-95=4412

Owner of vehicle: Busarus, Inc.
3798 Armenia Ave.
Tampa, FL 33677

Name of insurance co.: Motor Vehicle Ins. Co.

Make and model of vehicle: 1989 Plymouth Grand Voyager Van

Describe damage to vehicle: None

Names of persons injured: Susan Ames
1247 Carrollwood Lane
Tampa FL 33616

To what hospital were injured taken? NE Tampa General

Location of accident: In driveway of Brinkman School for the Impaired, at 12658 Northridge Drive, Tampa, FL

Describe severity of injury: ( ) killed (x) **serious visible injury ( ) minor visible injury ( ) no visible injury**

Describe what happened (indicate citation number):
(No citation issued.) Vehicle pulled into driveway of school to unload children. After getting off the bus, injured child dropped something under the front bumper of van and reached under van to get it. The operator thought all passengers were safely out of the way and proceeded forward running over her. Teacher standing in front of school yelled at van driver to stop but not before he struck the child.

Names and addresses of witnesses: Miss Clara Gump, teacher at Brinkman School. Her address is 9922 Orange Grove Avenue, Apt. 347, Tampa, FL 33615.

Investigating Officer: John Smith **Shield No.** 748

Appendix II

Hospital Medical Report in the Case of Ms. Susan Ames

DATE OF DISCHARGE: 5/3/92

SERVICE: Orthopedics

ATTENDING PHYSICIAN: Kenneth Jones, M.D.

PRINCIPAL DIAGNOSIS: Status post-motor-vehicle accident with bilateral shaft fractures, bilateral tib/fib fractures and bilateral petrous bone fractures.

PRINCIPAL PROCEDURE: Closed reduction, spica cast placement on 4-27-92. CT scan x2.

HISTORY OF PRESENT ILLNESS: The patient is an eight-year-old female pedestrian who was struck by a van traveling approximately twenty miles per hour. She was found unresponsive at the scene with a blood pressure of 70 and dilated left pupil. She was taken to Northeast Tampa General Hospital and was given crystalloid with increase of her blood pressure and intubated. Her vital signs remained stable.

Her C-spine, chest X ray, and pelvis were clear. The lower extremity films revealed bilateral femoral and tib/fib fractures. A head CT revealed a brainstem contusion. Abdominal CT was negative. She was transferred to Children's Hospital as a trauma. In our emergency room, she was initially stable, was awake, and was following commands.

In the emergency room, bilateral femoral pins were placed. She was put into traction. She was transferred to the pediatric intensive care unit. She was noticed to have abrasions throughout her head. She was intubated. She had blood in her nares. There was some bloody fluid coming from the right ear canal. The tympanic membrane appeared perforated. Her pupils were 3 mm. bilaterally, midline.

PHYSICAL EXAM: There was asymmetry of her gaze on initial physical examination. Her abdomen was soft. Rectal was guaiac negative. Pelvis was stable. She had obvious deformities of both lower extremities through the thigh and calves. Her distal pulses were Dopplerable bilaterally. Neuro: She was awake and nonverbal secondary to endotracheal tube. She opened her eyes spontaneously. She had decreased lateral gaze bilaterally. Upper extremities were 5/5 motor strength. Her lower extremity sensation was normal.

HOSPITAL COURSE: She was admitted to the PICU. She was seen by Orthopedics, Neurosurgery, Neurology, and ENT. She was placed in 90/90 traction. She had a baseline audiogram performed and a CT scan that initially showed some subarachnoid bleeding and bilateral fractures of the petrous bone. She also has bilateral 6th nerve palsy.

On 4-27-92 she was taken to the operating room where she had closed reduction of spica cast placement of her bilateral femoral fractures. On post op night her hematocrit was 33 and it dropped to 29. There was no active source of bleeding discernible. She continued to complain of double vision. Her spica was intact. Her distal motor sensory exam was intact.

The cast was windowed on postoperative day to view the wounds and also the right cast was wedged over the right tib/fib fracture and this was realigned. Repeat X rays showed this to be in satisfactory condition. Her official reading on the audiogram was a probable bilateral conductive hearing loss. She was also seen by Neuro-Ophthalmology, Dr. Brown, and ORL. Her drainage from the area stopped. She continued to be stable and on 5-3-92 was prepared for discharge.

FOLLOW-UP: Dr. Smith of Orthopedics in one week for evaluation of her extremity fractures. Dr. Brown and with ORL for a follow up audiogram.

Dictated by Kenneth Jones, M.D.

Appendix III

Exhibit A: Letter from the Plastic Surgeon in the Ames Case

Ms. Susan Ames was seen in my office in consultation with her parent on 5 June 1992. She had been involved in an accident on 27 April 1992, as the result of which she sustained compound fractures of both legs. Examination at this time revealed the following hypertropic scars and their approximate sizes:

a. Right leg 2.5 x 4.5 centimeters
b. Left leg 2.5 centimeters

Although there appears to be no neurological or functional involvement with these burn scars, the parent is unhappy with their appearance. It is my opinion that these scars could be made cosmetically more acceptable with excision and plastic surgical revision. However, this surgical revision should be delayed until ten to twelve months to give the scars time to mature. Despite the plastic surgical revision, she will always have residual scar tissue in these areas.

This procedure if performed would require a one-day admission to the hospital with standby anesthesia. My fee for this surgery would be $3,200.00

G.W. Miller, M.D., F.A.C.S.
Professor of Plastic Surgery
Children's Hospital Medical Center

Exhibit B: Letter from the Director of Pediatric Ophthalmology About Susan Ames

John Ames
1127 Henry Way
Tampa, FL 33620

Dear Mr. Ames:

I have been following your daughter's case since May 3, 1992. Susan developed bilateral sixth nerve palsies as a consequence of head trauma. The sixth nerve palsies innervate one of the muscles attached to the eye, which maintain correct alignment for the eye. Since the sixth nerve is responsible for turning the eyes out, the weakness that has been induced by the palsy has resulted in crossed eyes.

Despite marked improvement in the amount of palsy since the injury, Susan still has significant crossing of her eyes. Accordingly, we are planning to operate on the eye muscles to correct for the eye crossing.

Please feel free to communicate with me if you have any questions regarding Susan's care.

Sincerely,

David Lewis, M.D.
Director Pediatric Ophthalmology & Strabismus